best easy day hikes

Grand Staircase–Escalante & the Glen Canyon Region

Ron Adkison

FALCON®

HELENA, MONTANA

GET FALCON GUIDED

Falcon® Publishing is continually expanding its list of recreational guidebooks. All books include detailed descriptions, accurate maps, and all information necessary for enjoyable trips. You can order extra copies of this book and get information and prices for other Falcon® books by writing Falcon, P.O. Box 1718, Helena, MT 59624, or by calling toll-free 1-800-582-2665. Also, please ask for a copy of our current catalog. Visit our website at www. Falcon.com or contact us by e-mail at falcon@falcon.com.

CAUTION

Outdoor recreational activities are by their very nature potentially hazardous. All participants in such activities must assume responsibility for their own actions and safety. The information contained in this guidebook cannot replace sound judgment and good decision-making skills, which help reduce risk exposure, nor does the scope of this book allow for disclosure of all the potential hazards and risks involved in such activities.

Learn as much as possible about the outdoor recreational activities in which you participate, prepare for the unexpected, and be cautious. The reward will be a safer and more enjoyable experience.

 Text pages printed on recycled paper.

Contents

About the Author

Ron Adkison, an avid hiker and backpacker, began his outdoor explorations at age six. After more than 30 years of hiking, he has logged more than 8,000 trail miles in ten Western states. He has walked every trail in this guide to provide accurate, firsthand information about both the trails and features of ecological and historical interest. When he is not on the trail, Ron lives on the family's mountain ranch in southwest Montana, and with the help of his wife, Lynette, and two children, Ben and Abbey, raises sheep and llamas.

Ron shares his love and enthusiasm for wild places in this, his eighth guidebook.

Map Legend

Interstate		Picnic Area	
U.S. Highway		Campground	
State or County Road		Bridge	
Interstate Highway		Alcove	
Paved Road		Cabins/Buildings	
Unpaved Road, Graded		Ruins	
Unpaved Road, Poor		Ranger Station	
Trailhead		Elevation	X 9,782 ft.
Main Trail		Butte	
Secondary Trail		Dome	
Trailless Route, Wash Route		Cliffs	Top edge
River/Creek, Perennial		Falls, Pouroff	
Drainage, Intermittent Creek		Pass/Saddle	)(
Spring		Gate	
Forest/Wilderness/ Park Boundary		Overlook/ Point of Interest	
State Boundary	UTAH ARIZONA	Map Orientation	N
		Scale	0 30 60 Miles

Overview Map
Grand Staircase–Escalante & the
Glen Canyon Region

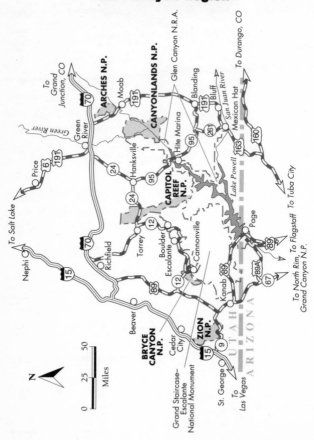

Introduction

The relatively undiscovered Glen Canyon region, stretching from Cedar Mesa near Blanding, Utah, to the Paria River Canyon near Glen Canyon Dam on the Arizona–Utah border, features hundreds of miles of excellent hiking and canyoneering routes in southern Utah. Within this region, hikers can enjoy outstanding canyon country landscapes with scenery rivaling that found in Utah's well-known national parks, but without the hordes of hikers that flock to those famous areas.

This handy guidebook, an abridged version of the comprehensive book called *Hiking Grand Staircase–Escalante & the Glen Canyon Region,* is the first book about the Glen Canyon region that meets the needs of day hikers, whether they are a family on vacation, or more serious hikers budgeting their time and energy.

The 19 easy hikes in this book survey the spectrum of the Glen Canyon region's landscapes: serpentine canyons and wooded plateaus, arches, natural bridges, Anasazi ruins, and rock art sites. The hikes range from less than a mile to 8 miles, although most are 2 to 3 miles in length. A few of the hikes have steep or sustained grades; most are gentle with minimal elevation change. Many of the hikes covered in this book are on well-defined, easy-to-follow trails. Only a few are trailless, and those routes follow canyon-bottom washes where routefinding skills are not necessary.

Ranking the Hikes

Easiest   Devils Garden
Wire Pass to Buckskin Gulch
Willis Creek Narrows
Cottonwood Canyon Narrows
Hog Springs Rest Area to Hog Canyon
Fortymile Ridge to Sunset Arch
Lower Calf Creek Falls
Mule Canyon
North Fork Mule Canyon
Kodachrome Basin State Park, Panorama Trail
Lick Wash
Collins Spring Trailhead to The Narrows
Kane Gulch Ranger Station to The Junction
Road Canyon
Willow Gulch Trailhead to Broken Bow Arch
Upper Calf Creek Falls
Government Trail to Grand Gulch
North Wash to Marinus Canyon
Hardest   Sipapu Bridge to Kachina Bridge

Maps

A variety of good maps covering the Grand Staircase–Escalante and the Glen Canyon region are useful not only for backcountry navigation, but also for navigation on the many remote desert roads accessing trailheads. Trails Illustrated topographic maps offer a good overview of two of the three regions covered in this book. For the Cedar Mesa region, use the Grand Gulch Plateau map (#706), and for the Escalante region, use the Canyons of the Escalante map (#710).

U.S. Geological Survey topo maps offer the most detailed representation of the landscape; although, they are not a necessity since getting lost while hiking in the bottom of a canyon is unlikely, especially when the wash is the only possible route. Yet for areas not covered by any other maps, such as the Grand Staircase, USGS maps are your only choice. The Bureau of Land Management produces a variety of 1:100,000-scale metric maps that will help you navigate through the Glen Canyon region. Hikers en route to and from trailheads in the Grand Staircase region should use the BLM Kanab and Smoky Mountain maps.

The Paria Canyon–Vermilion Cliffs Wilderness is covered by a black and white topo map showing the entire wilderness, but its scale of 5/8-inch per mile makes it most useful as an overview map. If hiking in the wilderness, either use USGS quadrangles, or obtain a copy of the Hiker's Guide to Paria Canyon, a BLM publication showing strip maps of all the canyons in the wilderness.

USGS topo maps, BLM maps, and Trails Illustrated maps are available at the Kane Gulch Ranger Station (open mid-March to October) and Natural Bridges National Monument on Cedar Mesa; at the Escalante Interagency visitor center and at Escalante Outfitters in Escalante; at the Kanab BLM office and Willow Creek Bookstore in Kanab, Utah; and at the Paria Contact Station between Page, Arizona, and Kanab.

Trails Illustrated maps and USGS quads covering the Escalante and Cedar Mesa regions can be ordered from the Canyonlands Natural History Association by calling 435-259-6003, or 800-840-8978.

Books and maps covering the entire Glen Canyon region can be ordered by mail from Escalante Outfitters in Escalante by calling 435-826-4266, or by fax at 435-826-4388. For the Grand Staircase and Paria Canyon, order books and maps by mail from the Willow Creek Bookstore in Kanab at 435-644-8884.

Zero Impact

The desert landscape of southern Utah appears deceptively durable, but actually it is very fragile. Once damaged, the desert recovers slowly and may not heal completely in your lifetime, if at all. Soils in this slickrock-dominated canyon country are thin to nonexistent. Plants and desert creatures balance delicately here to survive. The simple act of walking off the trail, even for short distances, can crush plants, move rocks, and otherwise disrupt this balance. Shortcuts and excavation at campsites hasten erosion of the thin soil cover, reducing and, in some instances, eliminating habitat for plants and animals. Shortcutting trails can also lead to the eventual destruction of a good, but perhaps unmaintained, trail.

Most canyon country hikers have long since learned to employ no-trace practices. Along most of the Glen Canyon region's trails and routes, and at its campsites, you will seldom find trash, food scraps, discarded items, soap suds in precious water sources, evidence of illegal campfires, or unnecessary excavations or alterations. Consider the following ideas for zero impact travel as guidelines for preserving the wilderness resource, not only for the desert's native inhabitants, but also for those who follow in your footsteps.

Waste

Garbage and food scraps attract animals, ants, and flies. Pack out your garbage and leftover food scraps with the rest of your trash.

Human waste must be deposited at least 200 feet from

campsites, trails, water sources, and drainages. Choose a spot with organic soil and dig a cat hole 6 to 8 inches deep, covering the waste with soil.

Do not bury or burn your toilet paper. Fires from burning toilet paper have devastated parts of the region; areas of Grand Gulch and Paria Canyon are examples. Some areas require that you pack out your used toilet paper, and most experienced canyoneers do, since decomposition does not take place in the desert. Zip-locked bags are useful for this.

Stay on the Trail

The passage of too many feet creates a lasting trail in the Utah desert, whether it be from campsite to water source or an off-trail route that can evolve into a trail. Use established trails where they are available. Your boot tracks in trailless areas will encourage others to follow.

Cryptobiotic Soil Crust

In some areas of the Glen Canyon region you will find large areas of soil covered by a black or gray lumpy crust. This delicate assemblage of mosses, lichens, blue-green algae, and fungi forms a protective layer against wind and water erosion, and aids in the absorption and retention of moisture, allowing larger plants to gain a foothold. The passage of a single hiker can destroy this fragile crust, and it may take 25 years or longer to redevelop. In areas covered by cryptobiotic soil crust, it is essential that hikers stick to established trails or follow routes over slickrock or sand.

Archaeological Sites

Evidence of ancient cultures abound in the Glen Canyon region, particularly on Cedar Mesa. Along some trails and routes, you are very likely to encounter archaeological and historical ruins and artifacts.

The majority of archaeological sites date back to between A.D. 1050 and A.D. 1200 (although evidence suggests occupation of the Cedar Mesa region as early as A.D 200), a time when the Anasazi widely occupied the region. Granaries, rock art, ruins of dwellings, potsherds, and chipping sites are among the cultural resources hikers may find in the Glen Canyon backcountry.

Keep in mind that these nonrenewable resources offer archaeologists insight into past ways of life in the region and can be easily disturbed and damaged by curious hikers. Although federal and state laws protect cultural resources, ultimately it depends on each of us to walk softly and treat these resources with the respect they deserve. Excavation and stabilization of many sites has yet to take place. Although hikers are likely to encounter many sites on trails and routes in the region, this book will not lead you to them, preserving for hikers the sense of discovery.

Ancient granaries and ruins are very fragile. Restrain the urge to enter or climb on their stone walls. Walk carefully around the slopes that support these structures. Ruins are best observed from a distance with the aid of binoculars. That way you will reduce your impact to zero. Areas with ruins are essentially outdoor museums, and visitors should conduct themselves as they would in any museum displaying irreplaceable artifacts. Ruins are an interesting highlight of a hike, but are inappropriate places to make camp.

After observing an archaeological site, move on before having meals. Food crumbs and garbage may attract rodents that could then nest in the site.

Pigments of ancient pictographs are easily destroyed by skin oils. Restrain the urge to touch them, particularly hand-print pictographs. Never add your own graffiti to irreplaceable rock art panels.

If you happen upon an archaeological site where artifacts remain, you may photograph them, but if you pick up or rearrange objects you may be destroying an important link to the past. Once an artifact is removed or disturbed, it becomes merely an object with little meaning to archaeologists. And, if you observe any unlawful or inappropriate behavior at archaeological sites, report the activity to the nearest BLM office.

The Falcon Principles of Zero Impact

• *Leave with everything you brought with you.*
• *Leave no sign of your visit.*
• *Leave the landscape as you found it.*

Play it Safe

All of the areas covered in this book are in wild, very remote country, far removed from enclaves of civilization. You must come prepared to be self-reliant, with a good attitude and ample supplies to deal with unexpected situations.

Hikers should note that hiking in canyon country is more

demanding than they might expect. Sandy washes and trails, cairned routes over slickrock, navigating among boulders, rock-hopping, and forging a way through streamside growth goes with the territory. Hikers new to canyon country hiking should take it slow and be careful until they grow accustomed to the rigors of travel here.

All hikers should carry at least two quarts of water per person on half-day hikes, and one gallon per person on all day hikes in hot weather. Avoid hiking in the Glen Canyon region during the hot summer months, but if you must, walk during the early morning and late afternoon hours only.

Always tell someone back home where you will be each day, and in the event you do not contact them at the end of your trip, make arrangements for that person to notify the county sheriff in your area of travel. Sheriff's phone numbers are listed for each chapter.

Be aware that road conditions and hiking conditions can change rapidly. Always obtain updated information on your route of travel from the BLM offices listed in each chapter. Flash floods can occur suddenly, leaving you stranded in canyons or on rain-slick dirt roads. Always be prepared with extra food, water, and clothing in the event you become stranded, whether in the backcountry or on the road.

You are allowed to bring your dog on the trail in all areas covered in this book, except in Grand Gulch downstream from the confluence of Collins Canyon and Natural Bridges National Monument. Keep your dog under restraint at all times, and never allow your dog to foul precious water sources. In Glen Canyon National Recreation Area, you are required to leash your dog. The desert is unforgiving to dogs not accustomed to the hot, dry environment. Carry extra water in dry areas, and offer it to your dog frequently. Hot rocks and sand will quickly burn your dog's paws, and dogs will overheat easily, so avoid bringing your dog in hot weather.

Cellular phones generally receive a good signal in the region, particularly in areas within sight of Kanab, Utah, and Navajo Mountain. Having a cellular phone with you will provide an extra measure of security in the event you run into trouble.

Items Every Hiker Should Carry

- At least two quarts of water per person
- First-aid kit (including bandages, moleskin, lip balm, sunscreen)
- Signal mirror
- Food
- Map
- Sweater or parka
- Rain gear, or windproof parka
- Hat with brim
- Hiking boots, lightweight and durable
- Toilet paper and zip-locked bag (for packing out used toilet paper)
- sunglasses

Cedar Mesa

Cedar Mesa is a broad, featureless plateau in southeast Utah, stretching north from Monument Valley and the San Juan River to the lofty tableland of Elk Ridge. Utah highways 95, 261, and 276 bisect this platform, where drivers are enveloped in pinyon-juniper woodlands and pass by unaware of the myriad canyons that cleave the mesa's surface.

The canyons of Cedar Mesa offer some of the most outstanding hiking opportunities in the Glen Canyon region, yet most of these gorges are overlooked by hikers en route to more well known southern Utah destinations. All of the canyons are carved into the mesa's namesake rock formation, the Cedar Mesa Sandstone, one of the most notable scenery producers in the canyon country of the Colorado Plateau. This resistant rock forms great bulging cliffs, often overhanging, resulting from the differential erosion of hard and less resistant beds of red and white sandstone. Hoodoos, spires of resistant rock sculpted by erosion, and mushroom rocks, a type of hoodoo shaped like a mushroom, typically punctuate the rims of the convoluted canyon walls.

Because of the Cedar Mesa Sandstone's response to weathering and erosion, great slickrock amphitheaters, cavelike alcoves and ledges dimple the canyon walls. It is in these hidden niches where people of the Anasazi culture long ago built their homes of rock, sticks, and mortar, and stored their grain. Ruins of this ancient culture and its mysterious rock art abound in the Cedar Mesa region, and each canyon here is virtually an outdoor museum of the culture.

Although the Anasazi people left their cliff-bound homes 700 years ago, many of their dwellings and granaries are so well-preserved it seems as if they left last week. An increase in visitation has led to the rapid deterioration of many sites, most often through the inadvertent impact of curious hikers. All visitors are urged to walk softly around these ancient archaeological sites (see the chapter *Leave No Trace*).

The nature of the Cedar Mesa Sandstone makes most hiking routes in the canyons very demanding and passable only to seasoned canyoneers. Yet there are exceptions, and the trails and routes described below are passable to any hiker. These hikes visit ancient ruins, outstanding lonely canyons, riparian oases, and natural bridges.

Camping

Only one developed campground is located in the Cedar Mesa region, and that is the 13-unit campground in Natural Bridges National Monument. This fee campground is open year-round, and is available on a first-come, first-served basis. It often fills by early afternoon in the spring and autumn, so arrive early if you wish to secure a site.

The campground is set in the pinyon-juniper woodland on the rim of White Canyon, and affords fine views into that slickrock gorge, and to the lofty prominences of Woodenshoe Buttes and the Bears Ears. Facilities include tables, tent pads, fire grills, and pit toilets. Water is available only at the visitor center, 0.25 mile from the campground.

If the campground is full or your vehicle exceeds 21 feet in length, use the overflow camping area, located 6.2 miles east of the visitor center. To get there, drive east of the monument to the UT 95/261 junction and turn right (south) onto UT 261. About 100 yards south of the junction, signs direct you left (southeast) down a gravel road to the camping area.

A private campground is located at Fry Canyon Lodge, 19.8 miles west of the UT 95/275 junction, the turnoff to Natural Bridges National Monument.

Most visitors to the Cedar Mesa region camp at-large, or wherever they wish, off the network of San Juan County roads that crisscross the mesa. Here, on public lands administered by the BLM, you will find almost unlimited opportunities to car camp in the pinyon-juniper woodlands. Most sites are short spur roads or pullouts, offering room enough to park and set up a tent. Always use established sites, and never drive off-road and create new sites. Extreme caution is advised if you choose to build a campfire.

Access and Services

Access to this remote region is provided by UT 95, a 121-mile highway linking Hanksville in the northwest with Blanding in the east, and is unquestionably the most scenic drive in the Colorado Plateau's canyon country. Cedar Mesa can also be reached via UT 261, which branches north from U.S. Highway 191/163, 4 miles north of Mexican Hat and leads 33 miles to its junction with UT 95.

Services are limited to the communities that lie far beyond Cedar Mesa. Groceries, gas, lodging, car repair and towing, and restaurants are available in Blanding, Bluff, and Hanksville. A medical clinic is located in Blanding. Fry Canyon Lodge offers the only gas between Blanding and the gas station/convenience store at Hite Marina on Lake Powell. The lodge also offers a cafe, six guest rooms, ice, propane, and a telephone for emergency use only. Pay telephones are available at Natural Bridges National Monument and at Hite Marina.

For more information on the Cedar Mesa region, visit the Kane Gulch Ranger Station on UT 261, 3.8 miles south of the junction with UT 95, or call the BLM San Juan Resource Area office at 435-587-2141.

In emergencies, dial 911, or call the San Juan County Sheriff at 435-587-2237.

1
MULE CANYON

General description: A half-day hike to an easily accessible canyon on Cedar Mesa, featuring several well-preserved Anasazi ruins.

Distance: 6 miles or more, round-trip.

Difficulty: Easy.

Trail conditions: Boot-worn trails and wash route.

Average hiking time: 3.5 to 4 hours, round-trip.

Trailhead elevation: 5,944 feet.

High point: 6,200 feet.

Elevation gain and loss: 250 feet.

Optimum seasons: April through early June; September through October.

Water availability: Seasonal intermittent flows in Mule Canyon; treat before drinking or bring your own.

Hazards: Flash flood danger.

Permits: Not required.

Topo maps: Hotel Rock and South Long Point USGS quads; Trails Illustrated Grand Gulch Plateau.

Key points:

0.0 Mule Canyon Trailhead.

3.0 Twin bays.

Finding the trailhead: Follow Utah Highway 95 to the signed turnoff of San Juan County Road 263 (Arch Canyon), lo-

Mule Canyon

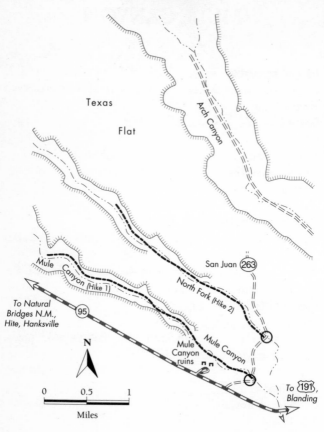

cated between mileposts 102 and 103. Find this turnoff 19.3 miles west of the U.S. Highway 191/UT 95 junction (3 miles south of Blanding), or 67 miles east of the Hite Marina turnoff, 9 miles east of Utah Highway 261, and 0.5 mile east of the signed turnoff to Mule Canyon Indian Ruins.

After turning northeast onto CR 263, pass a parking area on the right side of the road after 200 yards, then descend a short, but rough and rocky, downgrade to the bridge spanning Mule Canyon, 0.3 mile from the highway. A turnout on the right side of the road has room for two to three cars.

The hike: This pleasant, easy day hike follows the course of upper Mule Canyon, one of the most accessible canyons in the Cedar Mesa region. Great bulging cliffs of Cedar Mesa Sandstone embrace the canyon, which supports an interesting mixture of pinyon-juniper and montane forest.

The trail is sandy but well-worn and easy to follow with few obstacles, making it passable even to novice hikers. Typical of most Cedar Mesa canyons, you will see several well-preserved Anasazi ruins, most of them grain storage structures. Some ruins have direct access from the trail, while others are perched high on the canyon walls and can be observed only from a distance. All visitors must do their utmost to tread lightly around these fragile ancient structures.

From the bridge spanning Mule Canyon wash, follow either of two obvious trails that descend abruptly to the floor of the shallow canyon. There, the trails coalesce and quickly lead to the trailhead register. Beyond the register, the well-defined trail follows the edge of the Mule Canyon arroyo, soon crossing the often dry wash to the grassy bench on the opposite side.

The canyon is quite shallow at this point, flanked by low walls of Cedar Mesa Sandstone. Pinyon pine and juniper thickly mantle the cool, shadowed north-facing slopes to your left, while on the sun-drenched south-facing slopes, the woodland is open and sparse. Gambel oaks join the woodland trees in sheltered niches, and sagebrush and rabbitbrush form dense thickets on the deep alluvial soils of the benches that flank the wash.

After 1.7 miles, the first obvious draw opens up on the right (north). Beyond it, Mule Canyon grows deeper, flanked by red- and white-banded Cedar Mesa slickrock, with its characteristic bulging profile. Most of the ruins you will see are located above the draw.

After 2.3 miles, the trail winds among the pines, skirts a deep plunge pool on the right side, then the tread begins to deteriorate. A pair of bays, or shallow amphitheaters, open up on the north wall of the canyon after 3 miles, where tall cottonwoods crowd the banks of the wash. The trail essentially disappears around the point just beyond the twin bays, the canyon becomes increasingly confined, and a forest of tall conifers is amassed on the canyon floor.

Most hikers will be content to end the hike at the twin bays, and relax in the shadow of pines and firs, or soak in the sunshine on the slickrock before backtracking to the trailhead.

2
NORTH FORK MULE CANYON

see map page 16

General description: A half-day hike to a scenic Cedar Mesa canyon rich in Anasazi ruins.

Distance: 5.2 miles or more, round-trip.

Difficulty: Easy.

Trail conditions: Boot-worn trails and wash route.

Average hiking time: 2 to 2.5 hours, round-trip.

Trailhead elevation: 6,000 feet.

High point: 6,200 feet.

Elevation gain and loss: 200 feet.

Optimum seasons: April through early June; September through October.

Water availability: Seasonal intermittent flows in the wash; treat before drinking or bring your own.

Hazards: Flash flood danger.

Permits: Not required.

Topo maps: Hotel Rock and South Long Point USGS quads; Trails Illustrated Grand Gulch Plateau.

Key points:
0.0 North Fork Mule Canyon Trailhead.
2.6 End of trail.

Finding the trailhead: Follow driving directions for Hike 1 to Mule Canyon, then continue ahead on San Juan County

Road 263. The road is rough and rocky in places, yet it is passable to passenger cars.

After one switchback, you pass a parking/camping area, and after 0.4 mile you pass a corral and an undeveloped campsite. The road descends from the corral to the bridge spanning North Fork Mule Canyon, 1 mile from Utah Highway 95. Park in the wide spot immediately west of the bridge.

Hikers searching for a campsite will find numerous undeveloped sites in the pinyon-juniper woodland between Mule Canyon and the North Fork, and along the road beyond.

The hike: Much like the main fork of Mule Canyon to the south, the North Fork blends conifer forest and pinyon-juniper woodland with bold slickrock cliffs and easy access to a number of fine Anasazi ruins. This fork of the canyon is more confined, and many of its ruins, including dwellings, kivas, and granaries, are better hidden than in the main fork of the canyon, making a discovery more rewarding. Walking in the North Fork is easy and trouble-free. Segments of sandy, boot-worn trail guide you up-canyon, and in between you simply follow the wash.

From the southwest abutment of the bridge spanning the North Fork, a well-worn trail gradually descends northwest to the trailhead register. Although the North Fork is more confined than the main fork, the canyon is shallow, only 30 to 40 feet deep, for the first 0.5 mile.

The way ahead follows the small wash where, in spring, water will likely be flowing. You will follow segments of the trail, but most often you will be walking along the floor of the wash, with slickrock under foot, occasionally skirting boulders and plunging through willow thickets, forging your own way. Overall, the wash provides a clear avenue to follow up-canyon.

The bulging, often overhanging red- and gray-banded Cedar Mesa Sandstone cliffs gradually rise higher as you push deeper into the canyon, flanking the North Fork with convoluted 200-foot walls. After 1.9 miles, a prominent wooded draw opens up on the right (north). Just beyond the mouth of the draw is a deep alcove, crowned on its rim by a rust red sandstone knob. A seepline in the alcove supports a ribbon of hanging garden vegetation, including the brilliant blue flowers of primrose.

The trail essentially disappears after 2.6 miles. Most hikers will turn around here and retrace their steps to the trailhead, perhaps finding ruins they missed along the way.

3
KANE GULCH RANGER STATION TO THE JUNCTION

General description: A rewarding day hike into one of the Colorado Plateau's most famous canyons, within the Grand Gulch Primitive Area.

Distance: 8 miles, round-trip.

Difficulty: Moderately easy.

Trail conditions: Constructed and boot-worn trails, generally well-defined and easy to follow.

Average hiking time: 3.5 to 4.5 hours, round-trip.

Trailhead elevation: 6,427 feet.

Low point: 5,900 feet.

Elevation gain and loss: 530 feet.

Optimum seasons: April through mid-June; September through October.

Water availability: Perennial seep below pouroff at 2 miles; seasonal intermittent flows in Grand Gulch; seasonal Junction Spring a short distance below Kane Gulch/Grand Gulch confluence; bring your own water.

Hazards: Flash flood danger.

Permits: Required for overnight trips only.

Topo maps: Kane Gulch USGS quad; Trails Illustrated Grand Gulch Plateau.

Key points:
0.0 Kane Gulch Ranger Station.

2.0 Pouroff.

4.0 The Junction, confluence of Kane Gulch and Grand Gulch.

Finding the trailhead: From the Utah Highway 261/95 junction, 56 miles east of the Hite Marina turnoff, and 28.3 miles west of the U.S. Highway 191/UT 95 junction (3 miles south of Blanding), proceed south on UT 261 for 3.8 miles to Kane Gulch Ranger Station, located on the east side of the highway (the ranger station is also 29.2 miles north of US 191/163 between Mexican Hat and Bluff).

The hike: Beyond the confines of Utah's national parks, there are hundreds of outstanding canyons rivaling those within the parks in drama and beauty. And among these many canyons, Grand Gulch is one of the finest.

Grand Gulch is not only one of the most beautiful canyons in the Glen Canyon region, with its well-developed riparian oases and sculpted sandstone walls, it also bears the distinction of having one of the greatest concentrations of archaeological resources in a single canyon on the Colorado Plateau.

Kane Gulch Ranger Station is the jumping-off point for the majority of visitors to Grand Gulch, and the passage of so many hikers' boots keeps the trail well-defined and easy to follow. This short trip to the Kane Gulch–Grand Gulch confluence, called The Junction, not only offers a fine introduction to Grand Gulch, it affords access to the large cliff dwellings of Junction Ruin and several excellent campsites at the confluence. The trip is suitable as a day hike, an overnighter, or as the first leg of an extended trip into the

Kane Gulch Ranger Station to The Junction

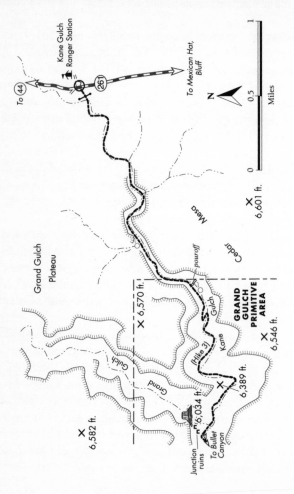

wild gorge of Grand Gulch.

From the Kane Gulch Ranger Station parking lot, find the trailhead on the opposite side of UT 261, indicated by a BLM destination and mileage sign. The trail crosses a sagebrush-studded flat for about 250 yards, then drops to the willow-and clover-fringed banks of Kane Gulch wash. Soon you pass through a gate (leaving it as you find it), cross an expanse of slickrock, then plunge back into the willows, where the trail turns to follow Kane Gulch down-canyon.

The gradually deepening draw soon becomes bordered by low walls of white Cedar Mesa Sandstone. Scattered cottonwoods and thickets of willow grow vigorously in the bottom of the gulch. Occasional bushwhacking through the willows here is more of a nuisance than it is a challenge.

After 2 miles, the trail bypasses a major pouroff on the right, then descends steadily over slickrock and a rocky tread back to the canyon floor. A line of seepage emerges from the slickrock beneath the pouroff, sometimes providing enough flow to dampen the wash below.

The trail, compared to canyoneering routes in nearby Cedar Mesa canyons, is pleasant and delightful. The nature of this trail allows you to simply hike and absorb the scenic landscape of this wild canyon, rather than constantly route-finding and picking a way around obstructions.

The gulch has attained true canyon proportions below the pouroff, and the rims now rest 300 to 500 feet above the canyon floor. The only vague segment of the trail ensues just below the pouroff, where you follow the wash down-canyon, with slickrock under foot. Soon, you mount another segment of constructed trail that stays high on the north wall of the canyon, following a ledge above a boulder jam and a series of minor pouroffs.

The only steep grade on the hike follows the traverse, where you descend the rocky tread back down to the slickrock wash below. Great alcoves and vaulting cliffs now flank the canyon, and the way ahead through this sandstone corridor alternates between stretches of well-worn trail over slickrock and sand, and brief trailless segments that follow the wash. There are few obstacles here to impede steady progress.

After 4 miles, Grand Gulch suddenly opens up ahead to the west at The Junction. Its upper reaches, slicing north back into the Grand Gulch Plateau, are quite similar in appearance to Kane Gulch. Straight ahead, Grand Gulch becomes a much wider canyon, flanked by benches studded with cottonwood, pinyon pine, and juniper. An excellent, though popular, camping area lies on a bench at the confluence while other sites are located just inside Grand Gulch to the north. The campsites, if unoccupied, afford shady resting places for day hikers as well.

Junction Ruin rests in an alcove high on the west wall of Grand Gulch just above The Junction. These well-preserved dwellings consist primarily of slab masonry construction, with one structure displaying wattle-and-daub architecture. To help preserve these ancient structures, hikers should be content to observe them from a distance, perhaps with the aid of binoculars.

After enjoying the peaceful beauty of The Junction, retrace your steps to the trailhead.

4
ROAD CANYON

General description: A memorable half-day hike into a Cedar Mesa canyon rich in archaeological resources.

Distance: 6.8 miles or more, round-trip.

Difficulty: Moderately easy.

Trail conditions: Boot-worn trail and wash route; occasional rudimentary route-finding required.

Average hiking time: 4 hours or more, round-trip.

Trailhead elevation: 6,390 feet.

Low point: 5,600 feet.

Elevation gain and loss: 800 feet.

Optimum seasons: April through mid-June; September through October.

Water availability: Seasonal intermittent flows in Road Canyon; treat before drinking or bring your own.

Hazards: Flash flood danger.

Permits: Not required.

Topo maps: Cedar Mesa North, Snow Flat Spring Cave USGS quads; Trails Illustrated Grand Gulch Plateau.

Key points:
0.0 Road Canyon Trailhead.
0.4 Enter Road Canyon.
3.4 First pouroff.

Road Canyon

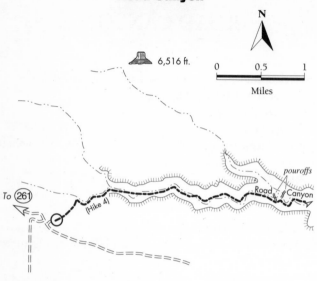

6,516 ft.

N

0   0.5   1

Miles

pouroffs

To (261)

(Hike 4)

Road   Canyon

Finding the trailhead: From the junction of Utah highways 95 and 261, 56 miles east of the Hite Marina turnoff, and 28.3 miles west of the UT 95/U.S. Highway 191 junction (3 miles south of Blanding), proceed south on UT 261 for 13.5 miles (or north for 23.5 miles from U.S. Highway 191/163 at Mexican Hat) to a junction with two dirt roads branching east and west from the highway. Turn east onto the road signed for Cigarette Spring (200 yards north of milepost 19).

This generally good dirt road, rough in places, should be passable to any vehicle in dry weather. The road leads

1 mile to a gate (leave it open or closed, as you find it), then becomes narrow and winding as it descends to an unsigned junction 3.4 miles from the highway. The right fork leads toward Lime Canyon.

Continue straight ahead (left) for about 100 yards, then turn left onto a northbound spur road. Follow the spur 150 yards to the road's end and unsigned trailhead, 3.5 miles from UT 261.

Hikers searching for campsites will find a few undeveloped sites near the junction with the road to Lime Canyon, and at the trailhead.

The hike: Road Canyon is one of a half dozen major canyons carved into the eastern flanks of Cedar Mesa and draining into Comb Wash. The canyon ranges from 100 to 400 feet deep, embraced by bulging walls of red- and gray-banded Cedar Mesa Sandstone sculpted into ledges, alcoves, sheer cliffs, and strange hoodoos. A seasonal stream fringed by a ribbon of riparian foliage, inviting benches shaded by a pygmy forest of pinyon pine and juniper, sculpted slickrock, and solitude provided by its remote, off-the-beaten-track location, offer ample incentives for visitors to seek out this canyon.

Yet the primary attraction of Road Canyon is not solely its natural beauty, but also its many very well-preserved Anasazi ruins and rock art that lure hikers here. Of course, I cannot disclose their locations. You must discover the ruins on your own. Much like nearby Grand Gulch, Road Canyon invites exploration. Allow plenty of time for the hike, perhaps an entire day, since you will likely spend more time here than you expect while scanning hidden recesses for ruins.

The ruins in Road Canyon (and those elsewhere on Cedar Mesa) are threatened by an increase in visitation. Simply walking around ruins inadvertently causes irreparable damage to the site. Several exceptional kivas in Road Canyon have deteriorated significantly since the 1980s due to human impact. Before visiting any ancient ruin, please read the chapter *Leave No Trace* in this book, walk softly when visiting ancient ruins, and treat them with the respect they deserve.

Begin at the road's end and follow the trail as it winds its way through the pinyon-juniper woodland, gradually descending across the mesa top. Please stay on the trail here to avoid crushing the well-developed cryptobiotic soil crust. After about 250 yards the trail begins a gentle descent above a wooded draw carving into the Cedar Mesa Sandstone. Here the woodland opens up to reveal the shallow upper reaches of Road Canyon below.

Soon you reach a steep, but brief descent of 120 feet to the boulder-littered floor of Road Canyon. Look for the cairn indicating this exit trail upon returning. Turn right and head down-canyon, where you will find segments of boot-worn trail. Most often, though, you will be walking in the wash, with slickrock under foot.

Boulders are amassed on the canyon floor at 0.6 mile, and cottonwoods and willow thickets appear as you follow trail segments through this rocky stretch. You must forge your way through the willows at times, but the thickets present more of an inconvenience than a challenge.

After you skirt a deep pothole in the wash, the northwest fork of Road Canyon joins on the left at 0.8 mile. After a few more bends in the canyon, a bold red hoodoo, capped by a gray sandstone slab, projects into the canyon from the north wall. Observant hikers will likely spot several ruins high on the canyon walls for the next 3 miles. As you continue down-canyon, narrow benches studded with pinyon pine and juniper begin to flank the wash, inviting you to return another time with overnight gear to pass a night or two in the canyon.

Although the walking is generally easy, there are places where you may have to stop and backtrack a few yards to find the best route around an obstacle, typical of canyon hiking in southern Utah. The canyon grows increasingly deeper as you proceed, flanked by 200- to 300-foot cliffs of convoluted sandstone, streaked with desert varnish.

After 2.5 miles, the serpentine canyon becomes much more confined, and you are eventually confronted by a typical Cedar Mesa pouroff, with a deep ephemeral pool below it, at 3.4 miles. Some hikers may elect to backtrack at this point, but if you are determined to continue to more ruins farther down-canyon, bear right and follow a shelf beneath an overhang, following a course that takes you well above the wash.

The route ahead follows the shelf for about 0.5 mile, beyond which a steep slickrock friction pitch and a brief downclimb are necessary to regain the wash. The canyon below is much deeper, with colorful, banded sandstone walls reaching 400 to 500 feet to the rims above. After 5.6 miles, just down-canyon from a northwest-trending side canyon, are some of the last ruins in Road Canyon. Most day hikers who have persevered this far will turn around at this point and retrace the route through this scenic canyon to the trailhead.

5
GOVERNMENT TRAIL TO GRAND GULCH

General description: An excellent, well-defined trail into lower Grand Gulch in the Grand Gulch Primitive Area, suitable as a day hike or as part of an extended backpack.

Distance: 6.4 miles, round-trip.

Difficulty: Moderately easy.

Trail conditions: Closed road to the rim of Grand Gulch, constructed trail into the canyon bottom.

Average hiking time: 3 hours, round-trip.

Trailhead elevation: 5,650 feet.

Low point: 4,880 feet.

Elevation loss: 770 feet.

Optimum seasons: April through early June; September through October.

Water availability: Seasonal intermittent flows in Grand Gulch; seasonal Pollys Spring emerges from inside Pollys Canyon, 0.2 mile north (up-canyon) of the foot of the trail; bring your own water.

Hazards: Flash flood danger in Grand Gulch.

Permits: Required for overnight trips; pay fee and obtain permit at the trailhead.

Topo maps: Pollys Pasture USGS quad; Trails Illustrated Grand Gulch Plateau.

Key points:
0.0 Government Trailhead.
2.7 Rim of Grand Gulch, beginning of Government Trail.
3.2 Floor of Grand Gulch.

Finding the trailhead: From the Utah Highway 95/261 junction, 56 miles east of the Hite Marina turnoff, and 28.3 miles west of the UT 95/U.S. Highway 191 junction (3 miles south of Blanding), proceed south on UT 261. You pass the Kane Gulch Ranger Station after 3.8 miles, where updated information on trail and road conditions is available. After 13.5 miles, about 200 yards north of milepost 19, turn right onto a westbound dirt road, opposite the turnoff for the road to Cigarette Spring.

Follow this road west for 0.4 mile where you find a gate (leave it open or closed, as you find it), a register, and an information signboard. The usually good, graded dirt road ahead has a few rough and rocky stretches, and barring severe runoff damage, it remains passable to passenger cars in dry weather. After 2.6 miles you reach a prominent, but unsigned junction, where you turn right.

This well-graded road leads west across the mesa, offering splendid views of Red House Cliffs, Tables of the Sun, Navajo Mountain, and the distant Kaiparowits Plateau.

You reach a signed junction after 3 miles (5.6 miles from UT 261), where you bear right onto graded San Juan County Road 245. Follow this road for 1.9 miles, then turn right onto a narrow spur road signed for Government Trail. This rough road has high centers in places, but remains passable to cars for 0.5 to 0.6 mile. Drivers with cars are advised to

Government Trail to Grand Gulch

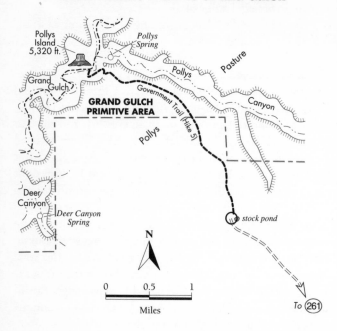

park in one of the wide spots on the slickrock at that point and walk the remaining distance to the trailhead.

Drivers of high-clearance four-wheel-drive vehicles can continue down the very rough and rocky road for the final 0.6 mile to the signed trailhead, 1.2 miles from CR 245, located next to a willow-fringed stock pond.

Hikers searching for a campsite have innumerable undeveloped sites to choose from en route to the trailhead.

The hike: Constructed by the BLM in the 1970s, Government Trail is the second shortest and easiest access into Grand Gulch. The way follows a long-closed road over the shrub-dotted expanse of Pollys Pasture, near the southwestern edge of the Cedar Mesa–Polly Mesa tableland, then descends 300 feet via a well-constructed trail into the middle reaches of Grand Gulch.

The hike is a rewarding day trip, but is most frequently used by backpackers as part of an extended trip in Grand Gulch. Although seasonal water sources are likely to be found in the gulch, day hikers and backpackers alike are advised to pack an ample water supply.

At the road's end, adjacent to the stock pond, you find an information signboard displaying maps, backcountry regulations, and abundant tips on leaving no trace.

Ample signs indicate the trail, which begins by crossing the dam of the willow-fringed pond. Just beyond, you curve left and skirt the bed of an abandoned Studebaker pickup truck. The first 2.7 miles of the way follows the doubletrack of a long-closed road, and signs at the trailhead ask hikers to walk in the left track only. Unfortunately few hikers do. As long as hikers keep walking in both tracks, the old road will remain a lasting, well-defined scar on the mesa.

Vistas from the mesa are far-ranging. The brick-red Bears Ears and Woodenshoe Buttes rise on the far northern horizon, defining the southern rim of lofty Elk Ridge. Moss Back Butte and the Tables of the Sun anchor the northern end of the Red House Cliffs to the northwest. The cliffs of Red Canyon, a prominent gap in the Red House Cliffs, frame a fine view of distant mounts—Holmes, Hillers, and Pennell—

in the Henry Mountains. And to the southwest, the sweeping ocher face of the Red House Cliffs point to the dome of Navajo Mountain, more than 50 miles away.

Midway to the rim of Grand Gulch, the road briefly disappears as you mount slickrock, where cairns point the way to the resumption of the double track ahead. Soon, overhanging cliffs come into view at the rim of Grand Gulch in the southwest, and Pollys Canyon to the north. After 2.7 miles of road walking, you reach the slickrock rim of Grand Gulch at 5,370 feet, where a large BLM sign proclaims Government Trail, Grand Gulch Primitive Area.

Here at last Grand Gulch opens up before you, a 300-foot-deep gorge embraced by sweeping walls of cross-bedded Cedar Mesa slickrock. Across the narrow gulf of the gulch rises the erosion-isolated butte of Pollys Island, cut off from the opposite rim by an abandoned meander of the Grand Gulch stream course.

The well-defined, constructed trail descends a moderate grade below the rim via switchbacks. In some places the trail is rocky, and in other places, the trail has been carved into the bulging slickrock. Six switchbacks lead down to the brow of a pouroff, where the trail turns left (southwest) and begins a lengthy traverse. Soon, a series of short switchbacks lead steeply down to the floor of Grand Gulch. Once you reach the gulch, you can roam at will. There is a wealth of archaeological sites here, but the Anasazi sites notwithstanding, Grand Gulch is arguably one of the most beautiful desert canyons in the region.

After enjoying your visit to Grand Gulch, retrace your route to the trailhead.

6
SIPAPU BRIDGE TO KACHINA BRIDGE

General description: A memorable half-day hike to the spectacular natural bridges of Utah's first national monument.
Distance: 5 miles, loop trip.
Difficulty: Moderately easy.
Trail conditions: Constructed trail, well-defined and easy to follow.
Average hiking time: 3 to 4 hours.
Trailhead elevation: 6,208 feet.
High point: 6,250 feet.
Low point: 5,640 feet.
Elevation gain and loss: 610 feet.
Optimum seasons: April through mid-June; September through October.
Water availability: Bring your own.
Hazards: Flash flood danger.
Permits: Not required.
Topo maps: Moss Back Butte USGS quad; Trails Illustrated Dark Canyon/Manti–La Sal National Forest.

Key points:
0.0 Sipapu Trailhead.
0.5 Sipapu Bridge.
1.2 Horse Collar Ruin.
2.6 Kachina Bridge.

Sipapu Bridge to Kachina Bridge

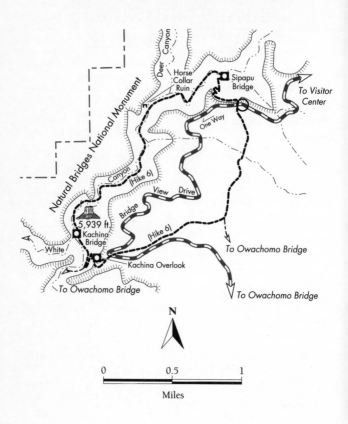

2.9 Kachina Bridge Trail; turn left.

3.3 Kachina Bridge Trailhead; cross the road to find the mesa trail.

4.2 Junction with southbound trail leading to Owachomo Bridge Trailhead; bear left.

5.0 Sipapu Trailhead.

Finding the trailhead: Follow Utah Highway 95 for 30.1 miles west from the U.S. Highway 191/UT 95 junction (3 miles south of Blanding), or 42.5 miles east from the Hite Marina turnoff, to northbound Utah Highway 275, prominently signed for Natural Bridges National Monument and Manti-La Sal National Forest–Elk Ridge Access.

This paved, two-lane road leads first north, then generally west, passing the turnoff to Elk Ridge after 0.6 mile, and the Deer Flat Road after 1 mile. You enter Natural Bridges National Monument at 3.8 miles, and reach the visitor center 4.5 miles from UT 95. Pay the entrance fee inside the visitor center before proceeding.

Beyond the visitor center you pass the campground and reach the 8.5-mile, one-way loop road, Bridge View Drive (open from 7 A.M. to 9 P.M. daily) after 0.5 mile, and bear right. The signed Sipapu Trailhead parking area is located 2 miles from the beginning of the loop road.

The hike: A visit to Natural Bridges National Monument is a must for anyone traveling on UT 95 across Cedar Mesa. Located near the head of White Canyon, a 40-mile tributary to the Colorado River carving throughout its length through the resistant Cedar Mesa Sandstone, the bridges in the Monument are among the largest in the world.

Cass Hite, prospector and operator of the Hite Crossing ferry on the Colorado River, claimed to have seen the natural stone bridges of White Canyon in 1883. J. A. Scorup, who ranged cattle across one of the largest ranches in Utah, visited the bridges in 1895. A later trip to the bridges guided by Scorup resulted in magazine articles that focused the nation's interest in preserving the unique landscape. President Theodore Roosevelt created Natural Bridges National Monument in 1908—the first national monument to be established in Utah.

The natural bridges of White Canyon were known by the Navajo and Paiute long before European settlers came to Utah. The Anasazi lived among the bridges in White Canyon, and hikers today visit the canyon not only to explore the unique natural spans of stone, but also to see Anasazi ruins and rock art.

This memorable half-day hike surveys the two largest of the natural bridges in the monument, separated by the dramatic bulging Cedar Mesa Sandstone cliffs of White Canyon. En route, the trail passes Horse Collar Ruin, an example of an unusual style of Anasazi architecture. The trail loops back to the trailhead via the mesa top, thus surveying the spectrum of monument landscapes.

From the Sipapu Trailhead, the trail begins as a rock-outlined slickrock route, descending over the White Canyon rim. The way quickly evolves into a constructed trail carved into the slickrock, with steps in place that afford better footing. Once below the rim, the trail traverses beneath an overhang to the top of a steel stairway that affords passage over an otherwise impassable cliff band. Tall Douglas-firs, a montane tree common on southern Utah plateaus above 8,000 feet, thrive in the cool microclimates of shady niches on the north-facing canyon walls below.

Soon you reach a second stairway that offers an exciting passage over a 20-foot cliff. Just below the stairway, descend a tall, sturdy wooden ladder, then follow the trail as it curves out to a fine viewpoint on a sandstone ledge at 6,000 feet, overlooking Sipapu Bridge. The trail then descends steadily, via switchbacks among Cedar Mesa slabs, upon slopes studded with pinyon pine, juniper, Gambel oak, and the spreading shrubs of Utah serviceberry.

You regain the slickrock below at the south abutment of Sipapu Bridge, which now towers above you. Descend two short but steep slickrock friction pitches with the aid of handrails and two short ladders, then reach level ground beneath the bridge in White Canyon wash, about 30 minutes and 0.5 mile from the trailhead. A trail register is located in a Gambel oak grove beneath the bridge, alongside the cottonwood-fringed banks of the wash.

The bridge was formed as the waters of White Canyon abandoned a meander in the stream bed and carved a more direct course through a thin wall of sandstone. This mature bridge, the largest in the monument, is no longer being enlarged by stream erosion, since its abutments now rest high above the wash. In its dimensions, Sipapu is second only to Rainbow Bridge in Glen Canyon, and thus bears the distinction of being the second largest natural bridge in the world. The bridge's dimensions are listed on the trail register.

To continue, cross the seasonal stream beneath the towering span of Sipapu, and follow the well-worn trail down-canyon, crossing the wash three more times en route to Deer Canyon. The trail ahead is a delightful walk through spectacular White Canyon. The bulging, mostly white walls of Cedar Mesa Sandstone present an ever-changing scene of sheer cliffs, alcoves, ledges, and towers sculpted into fanciful forms by ages of weathering and erosion.

Deer Canyon opens up on the right (north) 1 mile from the trailhead. Not to be missed is the short side trip to Horse Collar Ruin about 5 minutes and 250 yards below the mouth of Deer Canyon. A steep slickrock scramble is necessary to reach the deep alcove where you will find an unusual collection of small Anasazi dwellings and granaries.

Resuming your trek down-canyon on the well-defined trail, you will cross the wash five more times en route to Kachina Bridge. When you spy a small angular arch adjacent to blocky Ruin Rock on the southern skyline, only a few more bends of the canyon separate you from Kachina Bridge.

When you reach the bridge, you will notice a wooded draw branching left (northeast). That draw is an abandoned meander, the ancestral course of White Canyon, now resting several feet above today's stream course. Much like the formation of Sipapu Bridge, the stream abandoned its former course and carved a more direct route, creating the opening of Kachina Bridge in the thin wall of sandstone. Kachina is the youngest of the monument's bridges, and stream erosion is still at work enlarging the span.

There are multiple trails at Kachina Bridge. To stay on course, you should cross the wash twice beneath the bridge and head toward the trail register at the eastern abutment, where you will find a fine petroglyph panel.

After carving through Kachina Bridge, White Canyon begins a northwestward course toward its eventual confluence with Lake Powell. The trail, however, continues its southbound way, now ascending the White Canyon tributary of Armstrong Canyon. About 250 yards beyond Kachina Bridge, a small sign indicates the trail to the rim. With the aid of carved steps and handrails, begin ascending the slickrock to the left. Avoid the path that continues up Armstrong Canyon on the right side of the wash, since it soon dead-ends at a pouroff.

After the brief slickrock ascent ends, you traverse a short distance to a signed junction. The trail to the right continues ascending Armstrong Canyon, eventually leading to Owachomo Bridge. For now, bear left toward the Kachina Parking Area, gaining 300 feet in the following 0.5 mile, the steepest part of the hike. This trail ascends steeply at times, via rock steps and a series of short, tight switchbacks. Views expand with every step, revealing the red, layered Organ Rock Shale that caps the wooded mesas above. Although Kachina Bridge remains in view for much of the ascent, its angle of repose and shadows often give it the appearance of a large alcove rather than a great span of stone.

At length, the trail levels off as you curve around a bulging, mushroom-shaped knob just below the rim. Mount the slickrock, and ascend several yards to the paved Kachina Overlook Trail. Bear right and you will reach the parking area and loop road after 100 yards, at 6,032 feet. The trail resumes on the opposite (east) side of the road, winding over the corrugated mesa top with a gradual uphill trend.

Views from the mesa reach far down White Canyon to Mount Ellen in the Henry Mountains, to Deer Flat and the brick-red Woodenshoe Buttes in the northwest and north, and southwest to the square-edged platform of Moss Back Butte.

After 0.9 mile, turn left (north) at the signed junction, heading toward Sipapu Trailhead. Much of White Canyon disappears from view as you proceed north through the woodland. Be sure to stick to the trail while hiking across the mesa, otherwise the well-developed cryptobiotic soil crust will bear the marks of your passing for a generation.

Soon the northbound trail descends 120 feet into a prominent draw incised into the mesa. Enjoy the view to the twin buttes of the Bears Ears before dropping into the draw. Beyond the draw you briefly follow a steadily ascending cairned route over a broad expanse of slickrock, then resume your hike on a trail leading through the woodland.

At length, White Canyon opens up below you to the north, and you descend the final few yards to the Sipapu Trailhead.

7
COLLINS SPRING TRAILHEAD TO THE NARROWS

General description: A rewarding half-day hike in the Grand Gulch Primitive Area, leading to The Narrows of lower Grand Gulch.

Distance: 4 miles, round-trip.

Difficulty: Easy.

Trail conditions: Constructed and boot-worn trails, well-defined.

Average hiking time: 2.5 to 3 hours, round-trip.

Trailhead elevation: 5,080 feet.

Low point: 4,850 feet.

Elevation gain and loss: 230 feet.

Optimum seasons: April through early June; September through October.

Water availability: Seasonal intermittent flows in Grand Gulch; bring your own.

Hazards: Flash flood danger.

Permits: Required for overnight use only.

Topo maps: Red House Spring USGS quad; Trails Illustrated Grand Gulch Plateau; BLM Grand Gulch Primitive Area.

Key points:
0.0 Collins Spring Trailhead.
1.8 Confluence of Collins Canyon and Grand Gulch; turn right, down-canyon.
2.0 The Narrows.

Collins Spring Trailhead to The Narrows

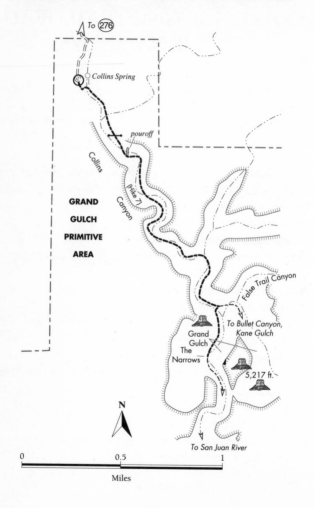

To (276)

Collins Spring

pouroff

Collins Canyon

(Mile 7)

GRAND
GULCH
PRIMITIVE
AREA

False Trail Canyon

To Bullet Canyon,
Kane Gulch

Grand
Gulch
The
Narrows

5,217 ft.

N

To San Juan River

0   0.5   1
Miles

Finding the trailhead: Follow Utah Highway 95 to the junction with southbound Utah Highway 276, signed for "Lake Powell," "Halls Crossing," and "Bullfrog via Ferry." This junction is located between mileposts 83 and 84 on UT 95, and is 83.8 miles southeast of Hanksville, 34.9 miles east of the turnoff to Hite Marina, and 37.7 miles west of the U.S. Highway 191/UT 95 junction (3 miles south of Blanding).

Follow UT 276 south across the rolling, wooded mesa beneath the Red House Cliffs. After leaving the woodland, the highway emerges onto a shrub-dotted terrace. You will pass milepost 85 6.4 miles south of UT 95. There, begin looking for a large, solitary juniper tree on the right (west) side of the highway. About 200 yards beyond the juniper and 0.3 mile beyond milepost 85, turn left (east) onto an unsigned dirt road. A BLM sign a short distance down this road points to Collins Canyon, and another sign designates the route as San Juan County Road 260 (Gulch Creek).

This good, graded dirt road affords memorable views of Navajo Mountain, Monument Valley, and the slickrock labyrinth of Grand Gulch. After 2.4 miles, bear right at an unsigned junction. Slickrock appears in the roadbed after 4.4 miles, making for a bumpy ride and dictating careful driving for hikers approaching in a low-clearance vehicle.

The road ends at the signed trailhead 6.5 miles from UT 276. Hikers arriving late in the day will find two excellent undeveloped campsites en route to the trailhead, or one may camp at the trailhead. In Grand Gulch, dogs are not allowed downstream from the confluence with Collins Canyon.

The hike: Grand Gulch, a rich riparian oasis and outdoor museum of the ancient Anasazi culture, is one of Utah's classic canyons. Yet its remote setting is largely reserved for the backpacker willing to spend several days exploring its hidden depths.

A notable exception is the easy walk down Collins Canyon to The Narrows, perhaps the best short hike in Grand Gulch. This fine trip traces the slickrock gorge of Collins Canyon, the only Grand Gulch access from the west, via a well-worn, and in places, constructed trail into the lower reaches of Grand Gulch. Unlike other Colorado Plateau slot canyons, The Narrows of Grand Gulch are very short, only stretching about 20 to 30 feet, but the canyon walls there are separated by only 8 to 10 feet. The tight confines of The Narrows often shade a shallow pool, making the slot an inviting destination.

From the trailhead on the rim of the mesa above Collins Canyon, exciting views reach into the slickrock-embraced gorge, luring you onto the trail that begins behind the information signboard and trailhead register. At once, the trail descends moderately via three short switchbacks over the first band of Cedar Mesa Sandstone and into the infant canyon below. There, you gently descend over the corrugated slopes above the draw of Collins Canyon.

Soon you pass the mouth of a shallow northeast-trending draw, and then pass through a wooden gate that bars cattle from entering Collins Canyon and Grand Gulch. Be sure to keep the gate closed. A brief, moderately descending segment of constructed trail, the steepest grade on the hike, ensues beyond the gate, dropping down a dugway into the wash below.

Upon reaching the wash, the tread becomes obscure. Simply follow the wash ahead for about 150 yards to the lip of a major pouroff. Cairns should be in place to direct you around the pouroff to the right (south) and onto another dugway, where the trail has been carved into the canyon wall. Another short, moderately steep grade leads you back to the canyon floor. Here you will notice the drainage has evolved from a draw just above the pouroff into a true canyon, now 200 feet deep.

Collins Canyon is presently embraced by tall, bulging, red- and tan-banded walls of Cedar Mesa slickrock. Domes, towers, balanced rocks, and sculpted hoodoos cap the overhanging canyon rims. Pinyon pine, juniper, and Gambel oak are scattered across the canyon floor, and occasional cottonwoods fringe the wash. Nearly every bend in the canyon presents a shady overhang, inviting a cool respite from the sun on the hike out.

After four bends of the canyon below the pouroff, the trail edges close to a small but distinctive arch. Be sure to take note of a north-trending side canyon that opens up on the left after 1.5 miles. Upon returning, bear left at that confluence, making sure that you do not turn into that canyon, which is similar in depth and appearance to Collins Canyon.

After rounding the next bend ahead, Grand Gulch opens up below, and soon you reach a shrub-studded bench at the mouth of Collins Canyon at 4,760 feet, 1.8 miles from the trailhead. There are two ways to reach The Narrows from this point. One route follows the rocky, sandy, and perhaps muddy wash of Grand Gulch down-canyon to the right (south) for 0.2 mile.

An easier way follows a boot-worn, occasionally brushy trail across the bench on the west side of the Grand Gulch wash. Find that trail from the mouth of Collins Canyon by heading south across the canyon's wash to the bench above. That trail dips into Grand Gulch just above The Narrows.

The Narrows appear suddenly and unexpectedly where Grand Gulch's stream has carved a passage through a narrow, finlike ridge, abandoning a long meander in the stream bed. The shade cast by the walls of The Narrows and its shallow, seasonal pool make this a fine peaceful destination on the sandy banks of the wash beneath the fluttering foliage of small cottonwoods. Great bulging cliffs soar 300 feet overhead, amplifying the music of the small, seasonal stream.

After enjoying this peaceful locale, retrace your steps to the trailhead.

8
NORTH WASH TO MARINUS CANYON

General description: A half-day hike through a seldom-visited, straight-walled canyon alongside Utah Highway 95 near Hite Marina and Lake Powell.
Distance: 7 miles, round-trip.
Difficulty: Moderately easy.
Trail conditions: Wash route.
Average hiking time: 4 hours, round-trip.
Trailhead elevation: 4,180 feet.
High point: 4,560 feet.
Elevation gain and loss: 380 feet.
Optimum seasons: Mid-March through mid-May; mid-September through mid-November.
Water availability: Bring your own.
Hazards: Flash flood danger.
Permits: Not required.
Topo maps: Hite North USGS quad.

Key points:
0.0 Mouth of Marinus Canyon on UT 95.
2.2 Forks of Marinus Canyon; follow right fork.
3.5 Reach pouroff and alcove.

Finding the trailhead: This unsigned, easy to miss canyon opens up on the east side of UT 95 in North Wash canyon, 0.4

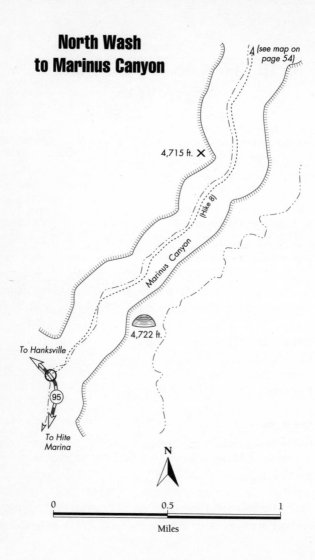

North Wash
to Marinus Canyon

(see map on page 54)

4,715 ft. **X**

(Hike 8)

Marinus Canyon

4,722 ft.

To Hanksville

95

To Hite
Marina

N

| 0 | | 0.5 | | 1 |

Miles

mile north of milepost 34, and 0.6 mile south of milepost 34. Find the trailhead by driving 34.6 miles southeast from Hanksville on UT 95, or northwest for 12.3 miles from the Hite Marina turnoff, and 1.7 miles north of the Glen Canyon National Recreation Area boundary.

A very narrow track leads about 100 feet across a small earth dam at the mouth of Marinus Canyon, but should be avoided. Instead, park off the highway in one of the wide spots near the canyon mouth.

The hike: South of Hanksville and west of the Dirty Devil River, between the sandy mesas of Trachyte and Cedar points, UT 95 follows the course of North Wash en route to Lake Powell and Hite. Passing through nine distinctive layers of progressively older sedimentary formations, featuring colorful clay beds, massive sandstone formations carved into sheer and fluted cliffs, and great amphitheaters scooped out of the canyon walls, UT 95 is one of the premier scenic drives in the Colorado Plateau region.

Three major tributary canyons, Marinus, Butler, and Stair, join North Wash alongside UT 95, and all of them offer grand scenery comparable to North Wash, yet few hikers bother to explore these cliff-bound gorges.

Marinus Canyon is a classic, dry desert gorge, embraced by fluted, 600-foot walls of Wingate Sandstone. The low elevations of the canyon make it a fine choice for an early spring or late autumn outing, when higher canyons, such as those on Cedar Mesa, are too snowy or cold. There are no trails here; simply follow the dry wash up-canyon. Although the wash route is generally easy and straightforward, the

Marinus Canyon

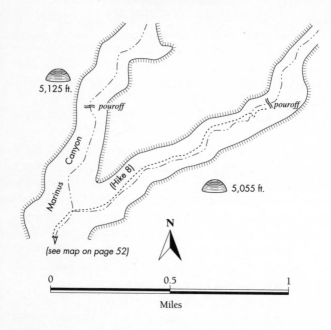

5,125 ft.

pouroff

pouroff

Marinus Canyon

(Hike 8)

5,055 ft.

N

(see map on page 52)

0   0.5   1

Miles

wash is sandy, and for much of the way you will be rock-hopping and weaving your way among boulders. At the end of the canyon's right fork is a shady overhang supporting hanging gardens, offering a fine destination for a half-day hike.

Enter the mouth of Marinus Canyon via the small earth dam, then simply make your way up the rocky, boulder-strewn wash. A scattering of Fremont cottonwood, tamarisk, and rabbitbrush fringe the usually dry wash, while apache plum, with its white spring blossoms and feathery summer fruits, and the green foliage of singleleaf ash dot the slopes above.

The wash begins amid the rocks of the Chinle Formation, and shortly after entering the canyon mouth you must briefly scramble up to the left of a resistant green ledge cutting across the wash, the only significant obstacle in the canyon.

Tall fluted cliffs of Wingate Sandstone, often coated with a metallic blue desert varnish, embrace the confined canyon, with the reddish brown ledges and cliff bands of Kayenta Formation rocks capping the rims. The lower slopes of the canyon are composed of the varicolored Chinle Formation rocks, the colorful beds hidden behind a mask of coarse desert shrubs and great sandstone blocks fallen from the cliffs above.

Vegetation in the canyon is sparse, and the scene is dominated by colorful sandstone cliffs. On occasion, Fremont cottonwood, seep-willow, and Gambel oak appear, joined at times by the rare appearance of a juniper. Spring wildflowers, by way of contrast, are abundant and decorate the stark canyon landscape with colorful blooms, including the vivid reds of scarlet penstemon and Eastwood paintbrush, the white mounds of desert peppergrass, and the fragrant lavender blossoms of collomia.

After gradually ascending this quiet, majestic canyon for 2 miles, you can see the confluence of two branches of the canyon a short distance ahead. Just before reaching the confluence, the wash is choked with huge boulders for about 100 yards. It is not too difficult to pick a way through this obstacle, with only minor scrambling necessary.

When you reach the forks of the canyon after 0.2 mile, at 4,275 feet, follow the right fork. In the left fork a boulder jam makes further travel difficult at best. The right fork ahead offers clear sailing, save for an occasional minor boulder jam and rock-strewn stretches.

Vegetation increases in abundance and diversity in this more sheltered, confined part of the canyon. Most notable are the many redbud trees, which put forth a brilliant display of reddish purple blossoms during April and May.

As you proceed, the Wingate Sandstone walls steadily close in and further confine the gorge. After passing above the top-most layer of the Chinle Formation, the Wingate reaches down to the canyon floor, and the drainage grows increasingly narrow as it slices back into this resistant sandstone.

After hiking about 1 hour and 1.25 miles from the forks of the canyon, you reach a low pouroff blocking further progress. Beneath the pouroff is a shady overhang, supporting a seepline decorated with the delicate fronds of maidenhair fern. During wet seasons, you will find a deep pool below the pouroff.

The canyon slots up ahead, and determined hikers can bypass the pouroff on the left and continue up-canyon. Most hikers, however, will likely be content to turn around at the pouroff and retrace their steps through Marinus Canyon to the trailhead.

9
HOG SPRINGS REST AREA TO HOG CANYON

General description: A short, easy hike to a lovely pool and waterfall in scenic Hog Canyon, alongside Utah Highway 95 near Hite Marina and Lake Powell.

Distance: 2 miles, round-trip.

Difficulty: Easy.

Trail conditions: Boot-worn trail and wash route.

Average hiking time: 1.5 hours, round-trip.

Trailhead elevation: 4,080 feet.

High point: 4,230 feet.

Elevation gain and loss: 150 feet.

Optimum seasons: Mid-March through mid-May; mid-September through mid-November.

Water availability: Bring your own.

Hazards: Flash flood danger.

Permits: Not required.

Topo maps: Hite North, Black Table USGS quads.

Key points:
0.0 Hog Springs Rest Area.
1.0 Pool and pouroff.

Finding the trailhead: The trailhead is located at the prominently-signed Hog Springs Rest Area, alongside UT 95 between mileposts 33 and 34, 15.2 miles northwest of

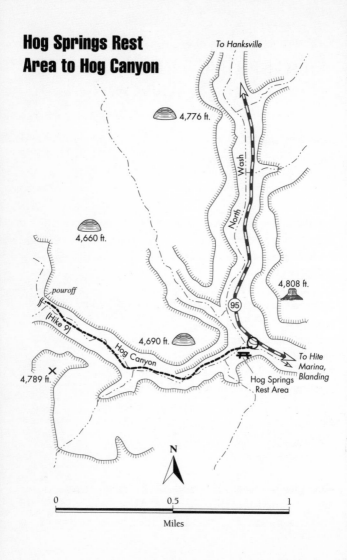

Hog Springs Rest
Area to Hog Canyon

To Hanksville

4,776 ft.

North Wash

4,660 ft.

pouroff

(Hike 9)

Hog Canyon

4,690 ft.

4,808 ft.

95

To Hite
Marina,
Blanding

Hog Springs
Rest Area

X
4,789 ft.

N

| 0 | 0.5 | 1 |

Miles

the turnoff to Hite Marina, and 33.3 miles southeast of Hanksville.

The hike: Hog Canyon is the principal drainage on the west side of North Wash along UT 95. The small, spring-fed stream, draining the eastern flanks of Trachyte Point, courses through the very scenic canyon embraced by the bold sandstone walls of the Glen Canyon group of rocks: the Wingate, Kayenta, and Navajo formations.

Located at the canyon's mouth alongside UT 95 is the Hog Springs Rest Area, a pleasant stopover featuring two picnic sites with awnings and tables, and a restroom nearby. The short stroll up Hog Canyon from the rest area offers a more intimate association with a dramatic desert canyon than scenic UT 95 can provide. One mile up the canyon, far beyond the noise of highway traffic, a deep pool and a small waterfall, lying in the shade of a deep alcove, offers an attractive destination for a short hike on a warm spring or autumn day.

From the large rest area parking lot, cross the bridge spanning North Wash and enter the picnic site. Immediately before reaching the second picnic table, follow the trail that descends to the banks of the small stream. Cross the stream and proceed up-canyon via the slopes above the wash on the right.

The trail begins as an obvious boot-worn path, but recent flash flood activity will determine how well-defined you find it. If the way is faint or briefly nonexistent, simply follow above the banks of the wash, shortcutting its meanders via stream-side benches. Avoid the rich growth of grasses and rushes where seepage creates a mire along the wash banks.

After 1 mile, you will hear the music of running water, then pick your way through a short, rock-strewn stretch of the wash to the source of that sound, hidden until the end behind a screen of tall willows. The wide pool lies beneath the overhang of a shady alcove, and a 6-foot waterfall, draining the perennial springs issuing from the upper canyon, plunges over a resistant ledge of Kayenta Sandstone into the pool. Mosses and fronds of maidenhair fern decorate the moist walls of the alcove, where seeping water drips like rain into the pool and onto the sandy beach beside it.

After enjoying this cool, peaceful locale, retrace your route to the trailhead.

The Escalante Canyons

The Escalante canyons are the premier hiking destination in the Glen Canyon region, and the reason can probably be summed up in one word: slickrock. From broad washes in the Circle Cliffs basin and on the Straight Cliffs/Hole-in-the-Rock terrace, and mountain streams high on the flanks of Boulder Mountain, the canyons of the Escalante River drainage quickly develop into a network of slickrock gorges that are the veins feeding the artery of the river. Although the Escalante River courses some 80 miles through a wilderness canyon of incomparable beauty, travel down its gorge is often brutal, a test of endurance for even the most experienced canyoneer. Its tributary canyons are equally attractive, and are the primary destinations of most hikers visiting the region.

Navajo Sandstone is the predominant rock formation in the Escalante canyons, and erosion has exhumed these ancient sand dunes and sculpted the resistant cross-bedded slickrock into a vast landscape of domes incised with innumerable serpentine canyons. Nowhere else in the canyon country of the Colorado Plateau is there such an immense expanse of slickrock. The unique landscape, reliable water in many canyons, and hiking routes that traverse the spectrum of difficulty, combine to make the Escalante region an increasingly popular alternative destination to the national parks of Utah.

The unique beauty of the Escalante region was recognized as early as 1866, yet the region somehow escaped achieving national park status in the ensuing years. After the floodgates closed on Glen Canyon Dam in 1963, the lower Escalante canyons were lost beneath the waters of Lake Powell. In 1972, the lower Escalante canyons were included within the boundaries of Glen Canyon National Recreation Area, managed under the direction of the National Park Service. With the establishment of the 1.7-million acre Grand Staircase–Escalante National Monument in 1996, and the modicum of protection that designation provides, all of the Escalante canyons are at last held in trust for the benefit and enjoyment of future generations.

Typical of the canyon country of southern Utah, there are few established trails in the Escalante canyons. Most hikes follow the corridors of washes, or cross open expanses of slickrock. The exception is the trail to lower Calf Creek Falls, one of the few constructed and maintained trails in the Glen Canyon region.

There are few easy hikes in the Escalante region, yet the few that qualify as best easy day hikes are outstanding. Active waterfalls, arches, narrow canyons, riparian oases, and sculpted slickrock are among the attractions of the Escalante's easy day hikes.

Camping

The only two public campgrounds in Grand Staircase–Escalante National Monument (as of 1998) are located in the Escalante region. The 5-unit Deer Creek Campground, located on the Burr Trail Road 6.2 miles southeast of Utah Highway 12 and Boulder, is open year-round and is available for a fee on a first-come, first-served basis. Set among willows and cottonwoods in the canyon of perennial Deer Creek, the site includes tables, fire grills, and pit toilets, but no drinking water.

The 13-unit Calf Creek Campground is located just off UT 12 at the Lower Calf Creek Falls Trailhead (see Hike 11). This fee campground is open year-round, and features the same facilities as the Deer Creek site, though drinking water is available from spring through autumn only.

Elsewhere in the monument or national recreation area, you may camp at-large, wherever you wish, unless otherwise posted. Roads en route to most trailheads offer spur roads or pullouts where you can park and set up a tent. Always use established sites, and never drive off-road and create new sites. Campfires should be avoided in the monument and are not permitted in Glen Canyon National Recreation Area.

Access and Services

The only highway providing access to the region is Utah Highway 12. This highway offers an exceptional scenic drive for 118 miles between UT 24 at Torrey, and U.S. Highway 89 south of Panguitch, Utah.

The historic Hole-in-the-Rock Road, branching southeast from UT 12 5 miles east of Escalante, affords access to the west side of the lower Escalante canyons. This is an often rough, remote desert road that is surprisingly busy with both hikers driving to and from trailheads, and scenic drivers.

Travel down this road is slow, so expect a drive of several hours en route to some trailheads. The road is subject to washouts, and can become impassable during and shortly after heavy rains. I have seen cars stranded on this road for several days following one afternoon of heavy rain. A four-wheel-drive vehicle is usually not required, but is recommended to safely navigate the road during changing weather conditions, though visitors drive the road in vehicles ranging from compact cars to motor homes.

Obtain up-to-date road information from the Escalante Interagency visitor center before driving this road, and be sure you top off your gas tank, and have several gallons of water, extra food, and other supplies in the event you become temporarily stranded.

Services in the region are limited to the small towns of Boulder and Escalante. Escalante offers gas, groceries, several motels, restaurants, hiking and camping supplies, auto repair and towing, and a medical clinic. In Boulder there are two gas/convenience stores, restaurants, motels, auto repair, limited groceries, and the Anasazi State Park and Museum.

For updated information on road and hiking route conditions, contact the Escalante Interagency visitor center at 435-826-5499, or visit the office at the west end of Escalante on UT 12. The visitor center is open seven days a week, from 7:30 A.M. to 5:30 P.M. from March 15 to October 31. Winter hours are from 8 A.M. to 4:30 P.M. Monday through Friday.

If an emergency arises, dial 911, or call the Garfield County Sheriff at 435-676-2678.

10
UPPER CALF CREEK FALLS

General description: A short but rewarding slickrock day hike in one of the upper Escalante canyons within Grand Staircase–Escalante National Monument.
Distance: 2 miles, round-trip.
Difficulty: Moderately easy.
Trail conditions: Cairned slickrock route and boot-worn trails.
Average hiking time: 1 to 1.5 hours, round-trip.
Trailhead elevation: 6,530 feet.
Low point: 5,920 feet.
Elevation gain and loss: 610 feet.
Optimum seasons: April through early June; September through October.
Water availability: Available at Calf Creek; treat before drinking or bring your own.
Hazards: Flash flood danger in Calf Creek canyon.
Permits: Not required for day hikes.
Topo maps: Calf Creek USGS quad; Trails Illustrated Canyons of the Escalante.

Key points:
0.0 Trailhead.
1.0 Upper Calf Creek Falls.

Finding the trailhead: The easy-to-miss spur road to the

Upper Calf Creek Falls

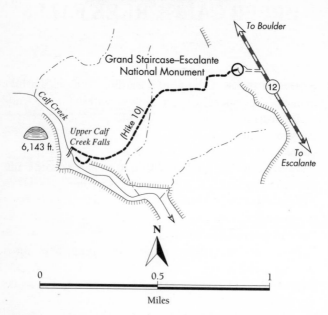

trailhead is located on the west side of Utah Highway 12, between mileposts 81 and 82, 5.5 miles southwest of the UT 12/Burr Trail Road junction in Boulder, and 22.4 miles northeast of Escalante. This spur road branches west 0.6 mile south of milepost 82, and 0.4 mile north of milepost 81. The very rough and rocky road leads 0.1 mile to the trailhead parking area on the rim of Calf Creek canyon. There are pullouts in which to park just off the highway if you are driving a low-clearance vehicle.

The hike: Few hikes in the Escalante region offer the rewards of this fine, short trip for such a minimal investment of time and effort. Vast expanses of Navajo Sandstone slickrock, far-ranging vistas, a tall waterfall, pools of cool water, and shady riparian oases await hikers following this well-worn trail.

Signs at the trailhead proclaim that no camping is permitted there, and that no camping or fires are allowed within 0.5 mile of the upper falls. The trail, leading immediately over the rim and to the top of a steep Navajo slickrock slope, begins behind these signs and the trailhead register. The slope is littered with round gray volcanic rocks and boulders. In fact, the slopes of all the upper Escalante canyons are strewn with these Tertiary rocks, carried in glacial meltwater from their source high on the slopes of Boulder Mountain more than 10,000 years ago.

A swath has been cleared through the rocky veneer, and cairns show the way down the swath via a moderately steep slickrock friction pitch. The route is easier than it first appears, and hikers should be confident that the slickrock affords good purchase.

Vistas from the start are dramatic and far-reaching, stretching to the Pink Cliffs of the Table Cliff Plateau on the western horizon, and far southwest to the Straight Cliffs bounding the Kaiparowits Plateau. Below you the drainage of Calf Creek unfolds, exposing miles of sweeping, cross-bedded, white Navajo slickrock.

Below the first short band of slickrock, a few minor switchbacks ensue, leading through volcanic boulders on a moderately steep downgrade to the next band of slickrock. Descend this sandstone slope, aiming for the obvious trail on the flats below. Once you reach this wide, well-worn sandy path, 300 feet below the rim, you begin a gradual descent over the sandy, gently sloping bench.

Shortly, the trail splits: the lower trail to the left descends over slickrock to the foot of the falls, and the upper trail to the right continues up-canyon to the head of the falls. Following the upper trail above the gorge, a lovely pool comes into view below, and behind it, a deep alcove rich with hanging vegetation. Then another pool, deeper and larger, appears. Finally you see the falls, an impressive veil of whitewater plunging about 50 feet over a sandstone precipice.

The trail leads to a small pool at the top of the falls, where Calf Creek's banks are fringed with a ribbon of willow, water birch, and silver buffaloberry. Scattered cottonwoods and ponderosa pines also occur in the canyon bottom, while slickrock slopes flank either side of the perennial stream. Just above the falls are a chain of small pools and deep waterpockets, irresistible on a hot day.

The lower trail descends slickrock, where there may be cairns to lead the way, for several hundred yards, to a shady alcove at the foot of the falls. Beware of the abundant poison ivy here, recognizable by its woody stem, 3 to 4 feet tall, and its large shiny green leaves, growing in sets of three. Here the music of the falls is enjoyed to its best advantage, and the large pool below is an added bonus on a hot day.

11
LOWER CALF CREEK FALLS

General description: A very scenic and popular day hike leading to a dramatic waterfall, within Grand Staircase–Escalante National Monument.

Distance: 6.2 miles, round-trip.

Difficulty: Moderately easy.

Trail conditions: Good constructed trail, sandy in places.

Average hiking time: 3.5 to 4 hours, round-trip.

Trailhead elevation: 5,320 feet.

High point: 5,500 feet at Lower Calf Creek Falls.

Elevation gain and loss: 250 feet.

Optimum seasons: Mid-March through early June; September through October.

Water availability: Available at the picnic site at the trailhead. Calf Creek supplies year-round water, but since it must be treated before drinking, bring your own.

Hazards: Negligible.

Permits: Not required.

Topo maps: Calf Creek USGS quad (trail not shown on quad); Trails Illustrated Canyons of the Escalante.

Key points:
0.0 Calf Creek Recreation Area day-use parking.
0.2 Trail begins on left (northwest) side of campground access road; bear left onto trail.
3.1 Lower Calf Creek Falls.

Lower Calf Creek Falls

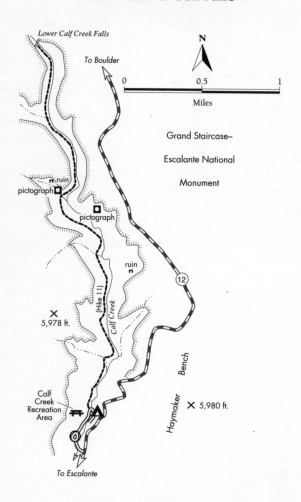

Finding the trailhead: The prominently signed BLM Calf Creek Recreation Area is located off Utah Highway 12, 11.4 miles south of the UT 12/Burr Trail Road junction in Boulder, 14.4 miles northeast of Escalante, and 1.1 miles north of the Escalante River bridge on UT 12. Follow the paved spur road for about 250 yards below the highway to the day-use parking lot. A small day-use fee is collected by campground hosts at the entrance to the parking lot.

The hike: This trip is one of the premier day hikes in the Escalante region, and for good reasons. An excellent self-guiding nature trail easily accessible from scenic UT 12, a pleasant campground located at the trailhead, a spectacular cliff-bound canyon, a perennial stream featuring beaver ponds and abundant trout, and a memorable veil of whitewater, one of very few active waterfalls in the southern Utah desert, plunging into a cold, deep pool, combine to make this trip a must for any hiker visiting the region. Lower Calf Creek Falls is a day-use area only; no overnight backpacking is allowed.

From the parking area adjacent to the picnic site, follow the paved road north through the campground for 0.2 mile, following signs pointing to the trail. Just before the road dips down to ford Calf Creek, the prominently signed trail heads left up the west slopes of the canyon.

As you proceed, refer to the brochure provided by the campground hosts as you entered the recreation area. It is keyed to 24 numbered posts along the trail, pointing out vegetation, geologic features, describing history and prehistory. The brochure will greatly enhance your appreciation

7 1

and enjoyment of the area. The actual distance to the falls is about 0.3 mile farther from the parking area than signs and the brochure indicate.

After reaching post 9, you mount the top most ledge of Kayenta rocks, then reach the Navajo Sandstone, the dominant formation in the Escalante region. Ahead, the canyon walls gradually close in, and sheer desert-varnished cliffs, capped by slickrock domes, dominate the canyon landscape. The creek bottom, however, remains a wide, verdant oasis, mantled in grasses, sedges, and rushes. In this part of the canyon, the trail passes through the shade of Gambel oak groves.

After about 2 miles, you reach the banks of Calf Creek for the first time, and the canyon floor ahead grows increasingly narrow. Boxelder, water birch, and Gambel oak mass their ranks on the canyon bottom and on the shady slopes just above. Now you can gaze into the clear waters of Calf Creek, brimming with fat brown trout reaching 12 inches in length, a rare sight in a desert canyon. The contrast here between the luxuriant riparian greenery and the stark profile of sandstone cliffs and domes is dramatic.

As you pass a chain of large beaver ponds you can hear the echoing crash of the falls long before you see it. As you round a bend, the falls appear, and soon thereafter you reach the trail's end in the confines of a slickrock amphitheater.

The memorable 126-foot fall plunges in one leap over the sandstone precipice above, then thunders onto a moss-draped slickrock wall and spreads a veil of whitewater into the deep green pool below. Relax here in a shady grove of water birch, or cool off in the deep pool in the spray of the falls.

12
DEVILS GARDEN

General description: An easy stroll through the erosion-sculpted sandstone spires of the Devils Garden Outstanding Natural Area, within the Grand Staircase–Escalante National Monument.

Distance: Variable, up to 0.7 mile.

Difficulty: Easy.

Trail conditions: Boot-worn trails and slickrock routes.

Average hiking time: Variable, up to 1 hour.

Trailhead elevation: 5,320 feet.

Elevation gain and loss: Minimal.

Optimum seasons: April through early June; September through October.

Water availability: None available, bring your own.

Hazards: Negligible.

Topo maps: Seep Flat USGS quad; Trails Illustrated Canyons of the Escalante.

Finding the trailhead: The prominently signed Hole-in-the-Rock Road, a BLM Scenic Backway, branches southeast from Utah Highway 12, 5.8 miles east of the Escalante Interagency visitor center in Escalante, and 23.8 miles southwest of the UT 12/Burr Trail Road junction in Boulder. Follow the good, wide, graded road southeast, passing a large destination and mileage sign a short distance from the highway.

Devils Garden

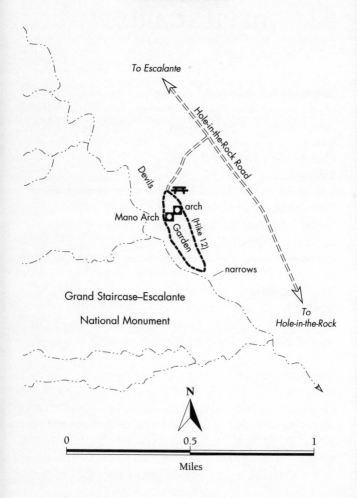

To Escalante

Hole-in-the-Rock Road

Devils

Mano Arch

arch

Garden

(hike 12)

narrows

Grand Staircase–Escalante

National Monument

To
Hole-in-the-Rock

N

0   0.5   1

Miles

Kilometer markers placed at 5 kilometer intervals (3 miles) allow you to gauge your progress as you travel this remote desert road. Always top off your gas tank and pack extra supplies before setting out on any desert road. After driving 10.5 miles from the highway, you pass the signed turn-off to the Harris Wash Trailhead. Continue south on the Hole-in-the-Rock Road for another 1.6 miles (12.1 miles from UT 12) to the signed spur road leading to Devils Garden, and turn right. Follow this often-rough gravel road for 0.25 mile to the spacious parking area adjacent to the picnic site.

The hike: The Devils Garden Outstanding Natural Area is an excellent place off the Hole-in-the-Rock Road for an afternoon picnic, followed by an hour or so of rewarding exploration. The garden is small, covering only about 200 acres, but it is a miniature wonderland of Navajo Sandstone hoodoos, domes, narrow passages, and small arches, hidden from the view of drivers along the Hole-in-the-Rock Road.

Devils Garden provides a brief introduction to the kind of slickrock walkways and trailless landscape typical of most backcountry routes in the Escalante region. Since the landscape features are in miniature here, obstacles, such as pouroffs and cliffs, are minor.

Devils Garden features a four-site picnic area with pit toilets, tables, fire pits, and elevated grills. No water is available. Bring your own firewood or charcoal, since firewood collecting is not allowed at the site. Dogs must be leashed at all times in Devils Garden. Although children will enjoy wandering with their parents here, remind your children to avoid trampling the coarse, yet fragile, desert vegetation.

There is no particular destination other than the garden itself, and there are numerous short, boot-worn paths to follow. You can strike out on your own over the slickrock, since everything here is on a small scale. It is easy to experience the entire area by wandering through it for an hour or so.

Miniature domes, tiny narrows carved by rivulets of infrequent runoff, and diminutive pouroffs are among the features you will see during your wanderings. There is a small arch spanning a gully that can be found by following the upper left-hand trail beginning at the picnic site. The lower trail skirts the base of Devils Garden's erosional formations, passing delicate Mano Arch and an array of red- and beige-toned sandstone hoodoos and mushroom rocks that rise from the pinyon-juniper bench. Other hiker-made trails criss-cross the area.

One can follow a short loop through the garden, covering about 0.7 mile along the way. The upper trail fades on the slickrock past the aforementioned arch, but you can continue over the sandstone slopes to a point above a bend in the wash, where it cuts through a 15-foot-wide slot. Loop back to the picnic site via the bench above the wash, skirting the dramatic hoodoos along the garden's western margin. Midway back to the picnic site, you will pick up a good trail to follow back to your car.

13
FORTYMILE RIDGE TO SUNSET ARCH

General description: A short cross-country day hike to an unusual mesa-top arch high above the lower Escalante canyons, within Grand Staircase–Escalante National Monument.

Distance: 3 miles, round-trip.

Difficulty: Easy.

Trail conditions: Cross-country route, rudimentary route-finding required.

Average hiking time: 1 to 1.5 hours, round-trip.

Trailhead elevation: 4,805 feet.

Low point: 4,520 feet.

Elevation gain and loss: 285 feet.

Optimum seasons: Mid-March through May; September through October.

Water availability: None available, bring your own.

Hazards: Negligible.

Permits: Not required for day hiking.

Topo maps: King Mesa USGS quad; Trails Illustrated Canyons of the Escalante.

Key points:
0.0 Water tank and trailhead.
0.1 Return to Fortymile Ridge Road, turn left (northeast).
0.2 Leave road at right-angle curve, next to a small water tank and concrete cistern, and bear right (south).

Fortymile Ridge to Sunset Arch

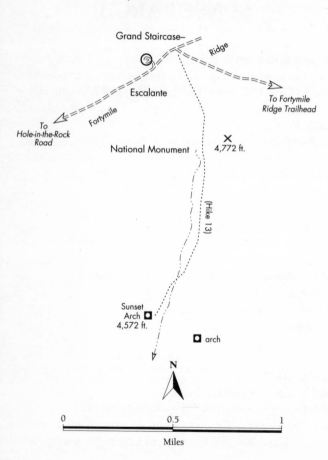

✕
4,814 ft.

Grand Staircase—

Ridge

Escalante

To Fortymile
Ridge Trailhead

To
Hole-in-the-Rock
Road

Fortymile

National Monument

✕
4,772 ft.

(Hike 13)

Sunset
Arch
4,572 ft.

◘ arch

N

0   0.5   1

Miles

1.5 Sunset Arch.

Finding the Trailhead: Follow driving directions for Hike 12 to the turnoff to Devils Garden along the Hole-in-the-Rock Road, and continue straight ahead. Although the hike to Sunset Arch is short and easy, the rough, bumpy drive to the trailhead will take 2 to 2.5 hours. Do not take travel lightly along this remote desert road. Come prepared with a full tank of gas, extra water, and extra food. Be advised that unexpected flash floods can wash out the road in places. When wet, the Hole-in-the-Rock Road can remain impassable, especially to two-wheel drive vehicles, for several hours to several days following heavy rains. Always check road conditions and weather forecasts at the Escalante Interagency visitor center before venturing down this road.

After 33.8 miles, you pass the signed Hurricane Wash Trailhead, then continue ahead for another 2.2 miles to the signed turnoff to Fortymile Ridge, and turn left (northeast). The narrow, sandy Fortymile Ridge Road typically develops a severe washboard surface along its entire length, though it is passable to two-wheel drive vehicles as far as the trailhead.

After 4.3 miles, turn left (north) onto the short, but steep, spur road that leads 0.1 mile to the trailhead adjacent to a large steel water tank atop the ridge.

Hikers searching for a place to camp will find a few pullouts along Fortymile Ridge Road, and many more undeveloped sites along the Hole-in-the-Rock Road.

The hike: Few hikers bother to visit Sunset Arch, a delicate, graceful span on the south slopes of Fortymile Ridge, which is surprising considering the accessibility of the arch via such a short and easy route. Most hikers who come to Fortymile Ridge are en route to one of two access routes into famous Coyote Gulch, north of the ridge.

Vistas along the way to the arch are far-ranging, and the walking is easy, with no obstacles. Yet there is no trail, and one is not really necessary along this straightforward route across the open terrain.

From the hilltop trailhead at the water tank, drop down to the Fortymile Ridge Road and turn left (east), walking another 0.1 mile to a right-angle bend in the road. Leave the road here, where you see a small steel water tank and concrete cistern, and follow a southeast course across the gentle, sandy expanse of Fortymile Ridge, heading toward prominent Point 4772 and its red slickrock slopes.

After about 10 minutes and 0.33 mile of weaving a course among blackbrush, sand sagebrush, mormon tea, and silvery sophora, you reach a minor drainage at the foot of Point 4772, then simply follow the drainage generally south, downhill. Broad vistas reach to the bold barrier of the Straight Cliffs and to the broad dome of 10,388-foot Navajo Mountain. Prominent features at the base of the Straight Cliffs include the isolated slickrock domes of the Sooner Rocks, and to the northwest of those domes you see an apron of Entrada Sandstone at the foot of Cave Point, where an array of deep alcoves create an intriguing contrast of light and shadow.

The better route ahead skirts the shallow arroyo of the drainage, rather than following its winding course. The left (east) side of the arroyo is much less sandy than is the right side. After about 1 mile, the arroyo ends when you reach an expanse of Navajo Sandstone slickrock. Using the distant Sooner Rocks as your guide, continue on your southbound course. Traverse the rolling slickrock for about 5 minutes and suddenly Sunset Arch appears on the low rim just ahead.

Angle upward to the small arch and relax in its shade and soak in the tremendous panorama. Sunset is a small arch, about 10 feet high, and stretching perhaps 50 feet between abutments. But it is a thin, graceful span, the eroded remnants of a dome of iron-rich Navajo Sandstone. A few past visitors, some as early as 1924, have left inscriptions in the arch. Please restrain the urge to leave your own mark behind.

True to its name, the arch faces west and frames a memorable sunset over the Straight Cliffs. Views reach south across the vast terrace traversed by the Hole-in-the-Rock Road, a landscape little changed since the members of the epic Hole-in-the-Rock Expedition pioneered the route in 1879 and 1880.

About 0.25 mile away, across the draw below to the southeast, you can see another small arch piercing a low dome of Navajo Sandstone.

From Sunset Arch, retrace your route to the trailhead.

14
WILLOW GULCH TRAILHEAD TO BROKEN BOW ARCH

General description: A half-day hike to a large natural arch in the lower Escalante canyons, located within Glen Canyon National Recreation Area.

Distance: 4 miles, round-trip.

Difficulty: Moderately easy.

Trail conditions: Wash route.

Average hiking time: 2 to 3 hours, round-trip.

Trailhead elevation: 4,200 feet.

Low point: 3,800 feet.

Elevation gain and loss: 400 feet.

Optimum seasons: Mid-March through May; September through October.

Water availability: Intermittent flows below confluence with Willow Gulch after 1 mile, but since it must be treated before drinking, bring your own instead.

Hazards: Flash flood danger.

Permits: Not required for day hikes.

Topo maps: Sooner Bench and Davis Gulch USGS quads; Trails Illustrated Canyons of the Escalante.

Key points:

0.0 Willow Gulch Trailhead.

0.2 Enter wash.

0.9 Confluence with Willow Gulch.

2.0 Broken Bow Arch.

Finding the trailhead: Follow the Hole-in-the-Rock Road for 36 miles southeast from Utah Highway 12 to the Fortymile Ridge Road (see driving directions for Hikes 12 and 13), and continue straight ahead, soon passing historic Dance Hall Rock. The road ahead undulates through several shallow drainages, and is often rocky, rough, and at times, steep and winding.

You pass the signed left turn to Fortymile Spring (the site of the Hole-in-the-Rock Expedition's camp during the winter of 1879–1880) at 37.5 miles, cross Carcass Wash at 39.4 miles, and finally, cross Sooner Wash at 40.5 miles. Several spur roads just beyond Sooner Wash lead to excellent undeveloped campsites among the Entrada Sandstone domes of the Sooner Rocks.

An unsigned road branches left (east) 1 mile beyond Sooner Wash, atop the desert terrace of Sooner Bench. Turn left here and follow the narrow track east. This road, which is occasionally rocky, with washboards in places, is passable to carefully driven cars. Enter Glen Canyon NRA after 0.6 mile, and reach the trailhead at the road's end after 1.4 miles, 42.9 miles from UT 12.

The hike: Willow Gulch offers one of the best short day hikes, also suitable as an overnight trip, in the lower Escalante canyons. The scenic route follows slickrock gorges sliced into a domed landscape of Navajo Sandstone. Interesting narrow passages, a ribbon of riparian foliage, beaver ponds in the small stream, and large Broken Bow Arch are major attractions.

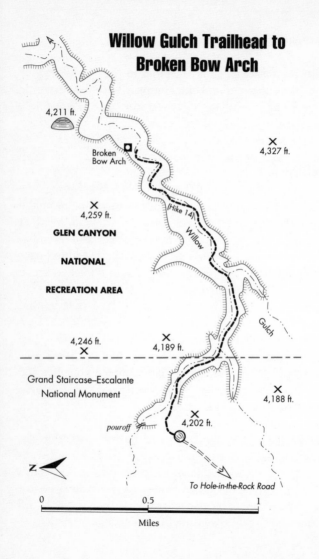

Willow Gulch Trailhead to Broken Bow Arch

4,211 ft.

Broken
Bow Arch

X
4,327 ft.

X
4,259 ft.

GLEN CANYON

NATIONAL

RECREATION AREA

(Hike 14)

Willow

Gulch

4,246 ft.
X

X
4,189 ft.

X
4,188 ft.

Grand Staircase–Escalante
National Monument

pouroff

X
4,202 ft.

N

To Hole-in-the-Rock Road

0   0.5   1

Miles

A well-worn path begins behind the trailhead register, descending a moderate grade down the sandy slope. Blackbrush, mormon tea, and sand sagebrush form a shrubby mantle over the sand slide. Also present is silvery sophora, a fragrant shrub with dense panicles of blue spring flowers that is a common denizen of sandy terrain. The beautiful canyon, embraced by desert-varnished walls of Navajo Sandstone, opens up 150 feet below.

Within moments you pass an interesting slab-crowned hoodoo, then bend east and descend slickrock and sand into the broad wash below. An intriguing stretch of narrows lies a short distance up-canyon, where the wash boxes up in an alcove decorated with hanging gardens. Once you reach the canyon floor, follow the sandy wash down-canyon, shortly passing a line of seepage fringed with the delicate fronds of maidenhair fern.

Soon the wash slots up, and most hikers bypass this slot by following a path above on the right (south) side of the drainage. The wash opens up again beyond that first constriction, but soon you are funneled into a passable stretch of narrows, beyond which you reach the mouth of a prominent side canyon that opens up on the right after 0.5 mile. On the left, a smaller draw joins the wash.

Continue straight ahead down the narrow, sandy stone hallway. Seep-willow and rabbitbrush fringe the wash, and soon, cottonwoods appear. As the wash grows damp ahead, a rich growth of cottonwood, willow, and seep-willow crowd the canyon bottom. The contrast between the cross-bedded, salmon-tinted slickrock above and the verdant riparian foliage is dramatic.

Soon, two paths begin following benches on either side of the wash as you approach the confluence with Willow Gulch, which joins on the right after 0.9 mile among tall Fremont cottonwoods. Turn left and follow Willow Gulch down-canyon. Water soon begins to flow in the wash, and evidence of beaver activity attests to the reliability of the flow. Willow Gulch opens up below the confluence, with grassy, brush-studded benches flanking the wash, and sheer desert-varnished cliffs and domes of Navajo Sandstone rising above. The canyon, however, remains fairly shallow. Rarely do the domes atop the rim rise more than 200 feet from the canyon floor.

After walking for several minutes below the confluence, a prominent trail forged by hikers wishing to avoid wading in the stream leads you up onto the right-hand bench. At length the bench pinches out, and you descend a minor gully back into the wash where you jump across the stream and follow a trail on the north-side bench, skirting a beaver pond.

Shortly, you return to the wash where the canyon grows increasingly narrow, bounded by bold cliffs and domes. Follow the twists and turns of the wash ahead, repeatedly crossing the small stream and tracing bypass trails above it. The stream is small but maintains a steady flow. In places it widens into pools and scooped-out waterpockets. Expect minor bushwhacking on occasion through thickets of limber willow and stiff tamarisk.

After curving around a prominent bend in the canyon, large Broken Bow Arch appears ahead. Cross the stream and follow the obvious trail up to the bench opposite the arch. The creek flows beneath a low overhang just below the bench, but a screen of Gambel oaks hide most of the stream-bed from view. From the bench, look for a steep, sandy trail that drops into the oak grove below. Do not continue following the trail on the bench, as other hikers have, because it deadends at an overhang and you will have to backtrack.

You regain the wash where an overhanging ledge, the top layer of Kayenta Formation rocks, shades the stream with hanging gardens of maidenhair fern directly below the arch. From here you can turn left, upstream, and scramble up to the arch, or continue down-canyon and approach the arch from the opposite side. Follow the base of the over-hang a short distance ahead to a bend in the canyon. A boot-worn path leaves the wash at the bend on the north side. Follow the path up to the bench, then head a the short distance up to the arch.

Piercing a thick fin of Navajo Sandstone that projects into the canyon from the north wall, the huge triangle-shaped aperture of Broken Bow Arch frames a memorable view of the convoluted canyon walls beyond. The base of the opening is heaped with great angular boulders fallen from above as stress fractures inexorably enlarge the span. The arch is shaded with a rich brown patina of desert var-nish. Tall, spreading cottonwoods in the wash below add a delicate contrast to the scene.

From Broken Bow Arch, retrace your steps to the trailhead.

Grand Staircase – Paria Canyon

The aptly-named Grand Staircase marches northward like a series of Brobdingnagian stairs, from the Arizona Strip to the 9,000-foot edge of Utah's High Plateaus. The colorful succession of "risers" in the staircase include, from south to north, the Shinarump Cliffs; the Vermilion Cliffs; the White Cliffs; the Gray Cliffs; and finally, the Pink Cliffs. Each cliff band is separated by progressively higher terraces, and all together this cliff and terrace landscape is remarkably uniform and quite unique. The Grand Staircase can be best viewed from a scenic overlook off U.S. Highway 89, between Fredonia and Jacob Lake, Arizona. From that vantage, the landscape to the north in Utah indeed resembles a staircase, and for people inclined toward hiking and/or scenic driving, it is an alluring landscape.

The Grand Staircase is the most remote, seldom-visited section of the Glen Canyon region covered in this book, though it is spectacular and contains the most extensive network of slot canyons in Utah. By way of contrast, the Paria Canyon–Vermilion Cliffs Wilderness, at the southwest corner of the Glen Canyon region, is so popular that annual visitation there almost outnumbers all other hiking areas in the region combined.

Comparable to other regions covered in this book, hiking in the Grand Staircase–Paria Canyon region is most often achieved without the benefit of a trail. Most of the easy day hikes follow dry, easily passable washes, leading through some of the finest narrows in the region. The exception is the excellent Panorama Trail in Kodachrome Basin State Park.

Camping

There are only two public campgrounds in this region. The 27-unit campground in Kodachrome Basin State Park (see Hike 15) is located 2.2 miles north of Cottonwood Canyon Road, 9.2 miles from Utah Highway 12 at Cannonville, Utah. This popular, scenic campground is open year-round and provides excellent facilities, for a fee, that include tables, water, fire grills, showers, a centrally located restroom, and a pay telephone. The sites are available on a first-come, first-served basis. Several sites can accommodate large trailers and RVs. A camper's store is located at Trailhead Station, next to the Panorama Trailhead, 0.5 mile from the campground.

The second campground is located at the White House Trailhead, the portal to Paria Canyon, 2 miles below the Paria Contact Station. Find this campground and trailhead by turning south onto a prominently signed dirt road branching south from US 89 between mileposts 20 and 21, 29.4 miles west of Page, Arizona, and 42.5 miles east of Kanab, Utah. Pay the appropriate fees and register for your stay in the campground at the information kiosk just off the highway, immediately below the Paria Contact Station, then drive 2 miles down the bumpy dirt road to the campground and trailhead.

White House is a small, walk-in campground, used primarily by Paria Canyon hikers. Its facilities include tables, fire grills, and pit toilets. You must pack out all your trash. No water is available, and there is a 5-person limit at each site.

Elsewhere in the region you are free to camp anywhere you wish on BLM-administered public lands, and there is ample opportunity to do so, particularly alongside the Cottonwood Canyon and Skutumpah (pronounced SCOO-tum-paw) roads. Please use established camping/parking spaces for car camping, and use extreme caution if building a campfire.

Access and Services

Two scenic highways, UT 12 and US 89, traverse this region from east to west. On the north, UT 12 (the only access to Bryce Canyon National Park) provides a 59-mile scenic link between Escalante and US 89 south of Panguitch, Utah. On the south, US 89 deviates from its usual north to south route and leads east and west for 71 miles between Kanab, Utah, and Page, Arizona.

On the extreme southern fringes of the region, mostly in Arizona, US 89A, yet another scenic route, is a 91-mile highway linking Kanab, Utah, with US 89, 23 miles south of Page, Arizona, and 100 miles north of Flagstaff. This highway, the only way to reach the North Rim of the Grand Canyon, provides access to Lees Ferry at the mouth of the Paria River.

Linking UT 12 in the north with US 89 in the south are two long, remote, and graded dirt roads: the Cottonwood Canyon Road, and the Skutumpah Road. Of these two routes, among the most scenic drives in Grand Staircase–Escalante National Monument, the Skutumpah Road receives more frequent maintenance and is the better road. The Cottonwood Canyon Road is subject to wash-outs and can be severely damaged by runoff from heavy rains. The road should be avoided in wet weather, when even minor rainfall renders its bento-nite clay surface impassable. Before driving either road, obtain an updated road report from the Kanab BLM office, the Paria Contact Station on US 89 between Kanab, Utah, and Page, Arizona, or from the Escalante Interagency visitor center in Escalante.

Both roads begin in Cannonville, on UT 12 in Bryce Valley, 23 miles east of US 89 (10 miles south of Panguitch), and 36 miles west of Escalante. The Cottonwood Canyon Road (of which the first 7.2 miles are paved) stretches 46 miles from UT 12 to US 89, 26 miles west of Page, Arizona. The Skutumpah Road leads 52 miles to US 89, 8 miles east of Kanab, Utah.

Kanab and Page are your best sources for whatever you may need while traveling through the region. Both towns offer a full range of services. On the north, the small town of Tropic, Utah is your only source of supplies between Panguitch and Escalante. Tropic offers five motels, gas, car repair and towing, restaurants, and groceries.

To obtain updated information, the Kanab BLM office provides a phone menu of recorded information, primarily on the Paria Canyon–Vermilion Cliffs Wilderness, at 435-644-2672. If you stay on the line, you can speak to a person and obtain site-specific information. Or you can visit the office by following signs that point to the office in Kanab. The Paria Contact Station is another excellent source of information if you are traveling between Page, Arizona, and Kanab, Utah, on US 89.

In the event of an emergency, dial 911, or contact the Kane County Sheriff at 435-644-2349.

15

KODACHROME BASIN STATE PARK, PANORAMA TRAIL

General description: An exceptional day hike leading through the colorful Entrada Sandstone formations of Kodachrome Basin State Park.

Distance: 2.9 miles, short loop; 5.4 miles, longer loop.

Difficulty: Moderately easy.

Trail conditions: Stage coach road and constructed trail, well-defined.

Average hiking time: 2 hours for the short loop; 3 to 3.5 hours for the longer loop.

Trailhead elevation: 5,780 feet.

High point: 5,960 feet.

Elevation gain and loss: 260 feet for the short loop; 360 feet for the longer loop.

Optimum seasons: April through early June; September through October.

Water availability: None available; bring your own.

Hazards: Negligible.

Permits: Not required.

Topo maps: Henrieville and Cannonville USGS quads (trails and state park not shown on quads; a trail map is available at the trailhead).

Key points:
0.0 Panorama Trailhead.

0.3 Junction with return leg of loop trail; bear right.

0.6 Stage coach road branches left; bear right onto the foot trail.

1.0 Junction with Big Bear Geyser Trail; bear right for the longer loop, or left for the short loop.

1.6 Junction with Mammoth Geyser Trail; stay right.

1.7 Junction with loop trail; bear right.

2.3 Junction with trail to Cool Cave; turn right.

2.4 Cool Cave.

2.5 Return to loop trail; turn right.

2.8 End of loop trail; bear right.

3.5 Return to Panorama Trail; turn right (south).

3.7 Foot trail merges with coach road; continue straight ahead.

4.1 Junction with return leg of Panorama Loop Trail (left), and Panorama Point Trail; bear right to Panorama Point.

4.3 Panorama Point; backtrack to return trail and proceed east.

5.1 Loop Trail junction; bear right.

5.4 Panorama Trailhead.

Finding the trailhead: From Utah Highway 12 in the Bryce Valley town of Cannonville, 33 miles east of Panguitch and U.S. Highway 89, and 36 miles west of Escalante, turn south onto Cottonwood Canyon Road (Cottonwood Canyon Scenic Backway), signed for "Kodachrome Basin–9." Follow this paved road south through Cannonville, then through the broad valley of the upper Paria River. You pass the junction with southwest-bound Skutumpah Road, leading to Kanab, after 2.9 miles, and after 7.2 miles, you reach the end of pavement on Cottonwood Canyon Road. Turn left here,

Kodachrome Basin State Park
Panorama Trail

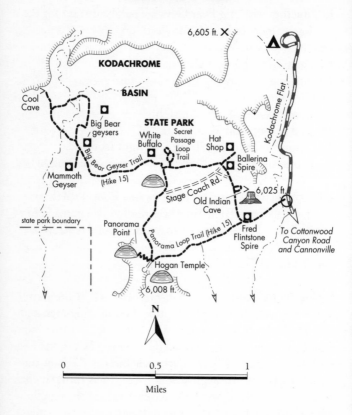

6,605 ft. **X**

KODACHROME

BASIN

Cool
Cave

Big Bear
geysers

STATE PARK

Kodachrome Flat

White
Buffalo

Secret
Passage
Loop
Trail

Hat
Shop

Ballerina
Spire

Big Bear Geyser Trail

Mammoth
Geyser

(Hike 15)

Stage Coach Rd.

Old Indian
Cave

6,025 ft.

state park boundary

Panorama
Point

Panorama Loop Trail (Hike 15)

Fred
Flintstone
Spire

*To Cottonwood
Canyon Road
and Cannonville*

Hogan Temple

6,008 ft.

N

0   0.5   1

Miles

staying on the paved road, to enter Kodachrome Basin State Park.

Stop at the self-service fee station (a modest day-use fee is required) after 0.5 mile, then continue north to a 3-way junction after 1.1 miles, where you turn onto the left-hand road, signed for the campground and scenic loop.

The signed Panorama Trailhead is located on the left (west) side of the road, 1.6 miles from the Cottonwood Canyon Road, and 8.8 miles from Cannonville. The 26-unit campground is located 0.6 mile from the trailhead, along the loop at the road's end.

The hike: Kodachrome Basin State Park, a 2,240-acre preserve southeast of Bryce Canyon National Park, is a place of vivid colors and dramatic landforms. Punctuated by the white chimneys of sand pipes, orange cliffs, spires, and finlike ridges of Entrada Sandstone that dominate the basin, it is one of the more spectacular areas in southern Utah, a land renowned for its unique landscape.

This state park is like a national park in miniature. Its concentration of unusual landforms, good access, numerous short trails, and visitor services that include a general store and campground, combine to make the park a premier destination.

Six hiking trails traverse the park, most of them less than 1 mile in length. The exception is the Panorama Trail, a nearly-level 2.9-mile loop that surveys what is perhaps the finest scenery the park has to offer. Panorama Point, an overlook just above the loop trail, affords an unparalleled vista across the park's colorful landscape. The 2.5-mile Big Bear

Geyser Trail can be taken to extend the trip into a rewarding half-day hike.

One mile of the Panorama Trail is shared by hikers, mountain bikers, and stage coach tours conducted by the park concessioner at Trailhead Station from Easter week through mid-October. The remaining single track is shared by hikers and mountain bikers only. The Panorama and Big Bear Geyser trails are the only trails open to mountain bikes in the park.

The sand pipes in the park add a unique dimension to a land dominated by unusual landforms. These white, chimney-like spires, averaging 30 to 50 feet in height, are composed of coarse sand that is far more resistant to erosion than the overlying orange Entrada Sandstone. Geologists believe that long ago the park was a geothermal area with hot springs and geysers much like Yellowstone National Park is today. After the springs and geysers ceased to flow, the area filled in with sand and left the white spires you see today.

The wide trail, narrower than a typical dirt road, begins behind the trailhead display sign, and traverses a grassy flat studded with juniper, big sagebrush, rabbitbrush, and four-wing saltbush. From the start, you are surrounded by an array of orange Entrada Sandstone spires. Other spires you will see along the trail are the white sand pipes, the resistant sediment-filled cores of ancient geysers and hot springs.

Many of the spires along the trail have been likened to familiar images and given fanciful names. Soon you reach the first, Fred Flintstone Spire, rising from bedrock, and just beyond it the trail forks after 0.3 mile, with the return leg of the loop branching left. Bear right, and quite soon you reach the first of several short spur trails, this one leading 100 yards to Old Indian Cave, a small, shady alcove. This trail is a loop, and shortly returns to the main trail.

The trail ahead traverses a gently contoured basin covered in grass and studded with the gnarled trees of the pinyon-juniper woodland. Fine views reach west to the Pink Cliffs of the Paunsaugunt Plateau in Bryce Canyon National Park. After 0.6 mile, the coach road branches left, and you follow the single track ahead where the sign indicates Panorama Trail. A tall, slender sand pipe, Ballerina Spire, rises a short distance north of the trail. You curve around it and soon reach the 200-yard spur trail to Hat Shop, a concentration of orange Entrada spires capped by sandstone slabs.

Beyond the Hat Shop, the trail traverses west across the open basin, bounded ahead to the west and southwest by a trio of large slickrock domes. The gentle trail passes through an open pinyon-juniper woodland where the flats are dotted with sagebrush and a variety of native bunchgrasses, including Indian ricegrass, needle-and-thread grass, and sand dropseed. As you approach the foot of the northernmost dome, you reach the Secret Passage Trail. That trail branches right, forming a 0.2-mile loop that includes the narrow slot of Secret Passage, and a view of White Buffalo, an unusual sand pipe formation perched atop the rim.

A short distance beyond the Secret Passage Trail, you come to the junction with the Big Bear Geyser Trail, branching right 1 mile from the trailhead. Hikers choosing to extend the hike will turn right onto that trail, following a brief steep descent off the ridge via badlands slopes. Below, you level off in a wooded basin, and skirt the base of intricately eroded 200-foot cliffs. Along this part of the trail you will capture glimpses into the canyon of the upper Paria River where it carves a gorge through the White Cliffs (Navajo Sandstone) of the Grand Staircase.

After hiking 0.6 mile from the Panorama Trail, you reach the signed spur trail that branches left, leading 0.1 mile to Mammoth Geyser, the largest sand pipe in the park. Another sand pipe, one of the Big Bear geysers, is visible on the rim of the cliffs north of the junction, and it can be viewed at a better advantage ahead.

Bear right at that junction, and quite soon you reach another junction, where signs point right and left to Big Bear Geyser Trail. Taking the right fork, you soon curve into an amphitheater where a 100-yard spur trail leads to the base of the cliffs atop which Big Bear Geyser rests. The trail ahead briefly becomes indistinct as it follows a small wash to the mouth of a precipitous slot canyon sliced through the cliffs just above. There, atop the rim, is the second of the Big Bear geysers, called Mama Bear.

The trail ahead follows the wash draining the basin until the wash curves east. Avoid the path leading into that east-trending canyon unless you wish to explore it. The main trail bends west here, skirting the cliffs for another 0.2 mile to the Cool Cave spur trail. Hikers will not want to miss this side trip.

The spur trail leads north into a small wash, which you follow up into an increasingly narrow slot. When the slot bends to the right, you reach Cool Cave, actually a deep alcove lying beneath a pouroff. Only a small patch of sky is visible overhead as the vaulting cliffs nearly envelop you.

Back on the main trail, the final 0.25 mile of the loop follows a gently undulating course across the basin, affording a long-range perspective of the Big Bear geysers. After closing the loop, backtrack for 0.7 mile to the Panorama Trail and turn right.

The Panorama Trail skirts the eastern foot of the first dome, then curves west around it, where the coach road and the trail merge. Just beyond the southern foot of the dome, a short spur trail leads to a fine vista point, where views unfold across the western reaches of Kodachrome Basin, including Mammoth Geyser, with a backdrop of the glowing Pink Cliffs.

Follow the coach road generally south toward Hogan Temple, the bold, convoluted slickrock dome straight ahead. The road soon skirts the second of the three domes, where you reach a signed junction. The coach road continues ahead and quickly ends in a loop. The return leg of the Panorama Trail branches left. If you wish to reach Panorama Point, turn right and ascend 120 feet in 0.2 mile, via a series of steep switchbacks. The point is actually the apex of a debris cone that mantles the eastern flanks of the dome.

From there, Kodachrome Basin spreads out in all of its colorful splendor. The basin below the viewpoint, with its velvety grasslands and pinyon-juniper woodlands, adds a soft contrast to the raw, rockbound landscape that surrounds it.

From the junction below Panorama Point, the return trail undulates across the basin for 0.5 mile to the junction, where you turn right and backtrack around Fred Flintstone Spire for 0.3 mile to the trailhead.

16
COTTONWOOD CANYON NARROWS

General description: An exciting short day hike through a narrow Navajo Sandstone canyon, located within Grand Staircase–Escalante National Monument.
Distance: 3 miles, round-trip.
Difficulty: Easy.
Trail conditions: Wash route.
Average hiking time: 2 hours, round-trip.
Trailhead elevation: 5,660 feet.
Low point: 5,500 feet.
Elevation loss and gain: 160 feet.
Optimum seasons: April through early June; September through October.
Water availability: None available; bring your own.
Hazards: Flash flood danger.
Permits: Not required.
Topo maps: Butler Valley USGS quad; BLM Smoky Mountain.

Key points:
0.0 Trailhead.
1.5 Mouth of narrows at Cottonwood Canyon Road.

Finding the trailhead: Follow driving directions for Hike 15 to the Kodachrome Basin State Park turnoff, then continue straight ahead on the graded dirt surface of the Cottonwood Canyon Road.

This road is infrequently maintained and subject to washouts. Throughout much of its course, this undulating, winding road traverses bentonite clay, which when wet, can become impassable, and at best, is very dangerous to drive. A high-clearance vehicle, preferably with four-wheel-drive, is recommended, though not required unless runoff has damaged the road.

After 1.5 miles, avoid a left-branching ranch road, and soon thereafter dip into the wash of Rock Springs Creek, fording its shallow stream. Enter Grand Staircase–Escalante National Monument 4.9 miles from the pavement, then ascend a steep grade to a saddle at 5.8 miles. Avoid the left-branching graded road immediately beyond the cattle guard at the saddle, and continue straight ahead.

A very steep grade soon leads down to the crossing of Round Valley Draw at 7.6 miles. You reach the junction with the signed left fork to Grosvenor Arch after 8.5 miles (15.7 miles from Cannonville). Few travelers forego the 2-mile round-trip drive to that unique arch and picnic site.

Continuing south on Cottonwood Canyon Road, you soon begin following The Cockscomb. The road crests a saddle 13 miles from the pavement, then begins an exceedingly steep downgrade into the drainage below. En route you can see the road cresting another prominent saddle 0.4 mile to the south. Between the two saddles at the bottom of the grade, the small portal of the Cottonwood Canyon Narrows opens up through The Cockscomb just west of the road. A small pullout on the left (east) side

Cottonwood Canyon Narrows

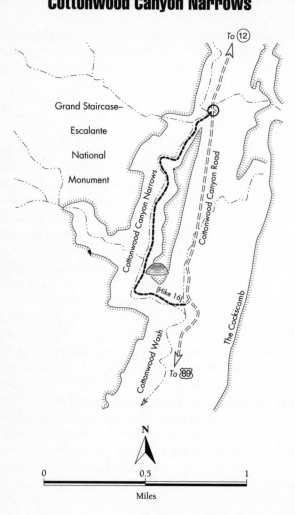

To (12)

Grand Staircase–

Escalante

National

Monument

Cottonwood Canyon Narrows

Cottonwood Canyon Road

(Hike 16)

The Cockscomb

Cottonwood Wash

To (89)

N

0   0.5   1

Miles

of the road affords the only available parking, 0.25 mile south of the north saddle, 250 yards north of the south saddle, and 20.5 miles from Cannonville. Another short spur road branches right 0.9 mile ahead, offering access into the mouth of the narrows.

The trailhead can also be reached from U.S. Highway 89 in the south. Find the southern end of Cottonwood Canyon Road (between mileposts 17 and 18) 2.2 miles east of the Paria Contact Station, or 26.3 miles west of Page, Arizona. The turnoff is indicated by a large BLM destination and mileage sign pointing to Cottonwood Canyon, Grosvenor Arch, and Cannonville.

As the road leads north away from US 89, it is sandy at first as it ascends over The Rimrocks. The road passes the Grand Staircase–Escalante National Monument boundary after 1.4 miles, then skirts the dramatic gray shale badlands at the foot of the Kaiparowits Plateau. After curving northwest to the broad valley of the Paria River, the road then begins to ascend the course of Cottonwood Wash.

Continue north along Cottonwood Wash to the aforementioned trailhead, 25.5 miles from US 89.

The hike: The Cottonwood Canyon Scenic Backway is perhaps the premier scenic drive in Grand Staircase–Escalante National Monument. Not only does the road afford access to well-known features such as Kodachrome Basin State Park and incomparable Grosvenor Arch, the road also follows The Cockscomb for many miles, one of the most unusual landforms in the monument.

Cottonwood Creek, an often dry stream, has over the

ages carved a long, deep, and winding canyon through the steeply-tilted rock beds of The Cockscomb. The creek ranges from the shadowed confines of narrow slots to a broad open wash. This fine short hike leads through the final narrow gorge of Cottonwood Creek before the canyon opens up and begins its long, straight journey to the confluence with the Paria River. The hike leads through the most easily accessible section of narrows along Cottonwood Creek, offering a rewarding, scenic diversion for anyone taking a drive down remote Cottonwood Canyon Road.

Opposite the small parking area, you will find a brown BLM post on the boundary of the 136,322-acre Paria–Hackberry Wilderness Study Area. From there, a path leads into the narrow wash just below, at the portal to Cottonwood Creek Narrows. There are three ways to enter: 1) follow the small wash for 50 yards down to an 8-foot pouroff, which requires one Class 4 move to get up or down; 2) just to the right (north) of the pouroff, a steep, rocky path descends briefly into the wash; or 3) a shallow draw, located about 100 yards north of the parking area, offers easy, trouble-free access into Cottonwood Creek.

Once you reach the wash of Cottonwood Creek, you may choose to turn right and explore the slot up-canyon. Chockstones and boulders make travel there challenging, and muddy pools persist in the gorge long after significant rainfall. Heading down-canyon, the walking is easy, passable to any hiker.

From the portal, the canyon bends west, briefly opening up. Soon thereafter, the canyon walls close in and you weave down the sandy, occasionally rock-strewn wash. Navajo

Sandstone cliffs embrace the gorge, standing 10 to 20 feet apart, and rising 200 to 300 feet above. The canyon walls are often sheer, in places overhanging, but fractures and ledges support a scattering of shrubs, and gnarled pinyon pines and junipers fringe the rims above. The canyon floor is also not barren, and here singleleaf ash, a small shrub-like tree, shares space with a scattering of Utah serviceberry, littleleaf mountain mahogany, and mormon tea.

Two precipitous slot canyons join Cottonwood Creek on the right, one ending in a shadowed amphitheater at 0.5 mile, the other at 1 mile. About midway through the narrows, an array of spires looms above on the western rim, and the gorge has reached a depth of 400 to 500 feet. After about 0.8 mile, you reach a prominent keyhole-shaped alcove scooped out of the right-side wall. In the autumn of 1997, a small chockstone blocked the wash here. If the chockstone is still present when you visit, bypass it on the left via slickrock slopes, or simply jump over it to continue.

As you approach the lower reaches of the narrows, the canyon begins to open up, and sandy benches appear. In response to increased sunlight and more available space, there is a marked increase in vegetation in this part of the canyon. Singleleaf ash mantles the benches, and is joined by rabbit-brush, Fremont barberry, pinyon pine, and juniper.

Near the end of the canyon, the wash describes a prominent bend to the east, and a small arch becomes visible high on the flanks of dome 5961 on your left, and soon several more skyline arches appear on the splintered canyon rim ahead to the southeast.

When the canyon bends east, it cuts through the steeply

tilted Navajo Sandstone of The Cockscomb, and once again you enter a narrow stone hallway. A boulder jam soon blocks the wash ahead, but there is an easy rock-strewn bypass route on the left side. Beyond that obstacle you exit the gorge and enter an open wash flanked by low benches clad in pinyon-juniper woodland. Do not be lured too far down the wash. When it bends south, you will see a pair of cottonwood trees just ahead. Leave the wash there and angle up to the left, soon following a path that quickly leads you to the short spur off Cottonwood Canyon Road. That spur offers an alternative starting point for a hike into the narrows.

From the road you can return the way you came, or turn left, and walk the road 0.9 mile back to your car.

17
WILLIS CREEK NARROWS

General description: An easy half-day hike through a dramatic narrow canyon in the White Cliffs of Grand Staircase–Escalante National Monument.

Distance: 4.8 miles, round-trip.

Difficulty: Easy.

Trail conditions: Wash route.

Average hiking time: 2.5 hours, round-trip.

Trailhead elevation: 5,980 feet.

Low point: 5,700 feet.

Elevation gain and loss: 280 feet.

Optimum seasons: April through mid-June; September through October.

Water availability: Seasonal intermittent flows in Willis Creek and Sheep Creek; treat before drinking, or bring your own.

Hazards: Flash flood danger.

Permits: Not required.

Topo maps: Bull Valley Gorge USGS quad; BLM Kanab.

Key points:

0.0 Willis Creek Trailhead.

1.3 Averett Canyon joins on the left (north); narrows end.

2.4 Confluence with Sheep Creek.

Finding the trailhead: From Utah Highway 12 in the Bryce

Willis Creek Narrows

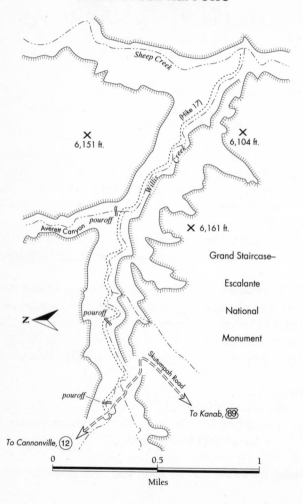

Valley town of Cannonville, 33 miles east of Panguitch and U.S. Highway 89, and 36 miles west of Escalante, turn south onto the Cottonwood Canyon Road signed for Kodachrome Basin–9. Follow the pavement through Cannonville, then through the broad valley of the upper Paria River. After 2.9 miles, Skutumpah Road branches right (southwest), signed for Bull Valley Gorge–9, and Kanab–61.

After turning right onto this road, the road immediately dips down to cross the Yellow Creek wash, then rises to the boundary of Grand Staircase–Escalante National Monument after 0.25 mile. After 3 miles you cross runoff below the spillway of a dam spanning broad Sheep Creek wash, ascend to a ridge, then drop down to the dry wash of Averett Canyon after 4.7 miles. After 5.5 miles, avoid a graded road that branches right near the crest of a ridge. Bear left there and descend to the wash of Willis Creek, 6.3 miles from Cottonwood Canyon Road. Parking is available on either side of the wash.

The trailhead is also accessible from US 89 in the south. From US 89, turn north where a sign indicates Johnson Canyon, immediately east of milepost 55, and 8 miles east of Kanab, Utah, or 64 miles west of Page, Arizona. Follow this paved road as it gradually ascends Johnson Canyon for 16.2 miles to a signed junction. At the junction, turn right onto the good gravel road (Skutumpah Road), signed for Deer Springs Ranch and Cannonville.

After driving 11.5 miles from the junction, avoid several signed spur roads for 0.2 mile, leading to the private property of Deer Springs Ranch. You reach Willis Creek wash 26.5 miles from the pavement, and 42.7 miles from US 89.

Drivers approaching from either direction will find numerous undeveloped campsites in the pinyon-juniper woodland, many with fine views of the Pink Cliffs of Bryce Canyon National Park.

The hike: Some of the most dramatic slot canyons in the world have been carved into the White Cliffs of the Grand Staircase in southern Utah. Many of these slot canyons are accessible only to veteran canyoneers well-versed in a variety of rock climbing techniques.

Yet there are slot canyons that involve no more than a pleasant walk down their shadowed stone hallways. Willis Creek is such a canyon. Born on the flanks of the Pink Cliffs in Bryce Canyon National Park, the broad wash of Willis Creek carves a swath through densely wooded terraces until it reaches the Navajo Sandstone of the White Cliffs. There, the wash seems to disappear, becoming entrenched between 200- to 300-foot slickrock walls. This gorge, with many narrow passages, stretches 2.4 miles down to its confluence with much larger Sheep Creek canyon, another Pink Cliffs drainage.

On this fine short hike there is no particular destination other than the narrows of Willis Creek. Go as far as you wish; the best narrows are found along the first 1.3 miles.

Where the broad wash of Willis Creek crosses the Skutumpah Road, there is little intimation of a narrow gorge below. Cross the road and follow the wash downstream. Quite soon the Navajo Sandstone emerges and the wash immediately slots up. Scramble down into the wash just below a low pouroff and proceed down-canyon.

At first, the Navajo cliffs are low but confining. The occasional appearance of ponderosa pines allows you to judge the height of the canyon walls. After following a few bends of the developing canyon, the walls suddenly rise higher, and you are funneled into a slot where only 6 to 10 feet of space separate the slickrock walls. Although there may be a very small, shallow stream in the upper reaches of the gorge during early spring or following extended periods of rainfall, most of the hike passes over the dry gravel wash.

After 0.6 mile, you reach another pouroff, easily bypassed via the slickrock ledge on the left side. The drainage of Averett Canyon, entering on the left via a rugged gorge, opens up after 1.3 miles. That canyon was named in honor of Elijah Averett, a member of a party of Utah Territorial Militia in search of Indian raiders who killed settlers in Long Valley, near the town of Glendale, in the spring of 1866. Averett himself was killed by Indian rifles in August of 1866, while crossing the canyon that now bears his name.

There are no more slots below Averett Canyon, though Willis Creek remains to be a confined, spectacular canyon, and the walking is easy over the wide gravel wash. When you see a 200-foot cliff apparently blocking your way ahead, you are only minutes from the confluence with Sheep Creek wash. From Sheep Creek at 2.4 miles, backtrack through the shadowed gorge to the trailhead.

18
LICK WASH

General description: An excellent day hike through a deep and narrow canyon in the Grand Staircase, located within Grand Staircase–Escalante National Monument.

Distance: 8 miles, round-trip.

Difficulty: Moderately easy.

Trail conditions: Wash route.

Average hiking time: 4 hours, round trip.

Trailhead elevation: 6,330 feet.

Low point: 6,000 feet.

Elevation loss and gain: 330 feet.

Optimum seasons: April through mid-June; September through October.

Water availability: None available; bring your own.

Hazards: Flash flood danger.

Permits: Not required.

Topo maps: Deer Spring Point USGS quad; BLM Kanab.

Key points:
0.0 Trailhead.
4.0 Park Wash.

Finding the trailhead: Drivers coming from Utah Highway 12 in the north should follow driving directions for Hike 17 to Willis Creek, 9.2 miles southwest of Cannonville via the

Cottonwood Canyon and Skutumpah roads, and continue straight ahead on Skutumpah Road. After 10.9 miles, the road crosses the narrow bridge spanning cavernous Bull Valley Gorge. Enter signed Bullrush Hollow after 16.9 miles, and enjoy the first good views of the towering White Cliffs in the southern distance. After emerging from the woodland at 18.6 miles, you enter the broad, brushy basin of Dry Valley, then gradually descend to an unsigned crossing of Lick Wash at 19.9 miles, where the road is subject to washouts. A short distance beyond the wash, immediately before reaching a cattle guard, turn left onto a faint spur road. Follow the spur for 0.1 mile to its end above the banks of Lick Wash and park there.

From U.S. Highway 89 in the south, you can find the trailhead by turning north where a sign indicates Johnson Canyon. This turnoff is located immediately east of milepost 55, and 8 miles east of Kanab, Utah, or 64 miles west of Page, Arizona. Follow the paved Johnson Canyon Road north for 16.2 miles to a signed junction, then turn right onto the good gravel Skutumpah Road, signed for Deer Springs Ranch and Cannonville.

Avoid several signed spur roads leading to the private property of the Deer Springs Ranch between 11.5 and 11.7 miles from the junction. After driving 14.8 miles from the junction at the end of the pavement (31 miles from US 89), you reach the aforementioned spur road leading to the trailhead, just before the Skutumpah Road crosses Lick Wash.

The hike: Lick Wash is one of many largely unknown, uncelebrated canyons carved into the remote White Cliffs

113

Lick Wash

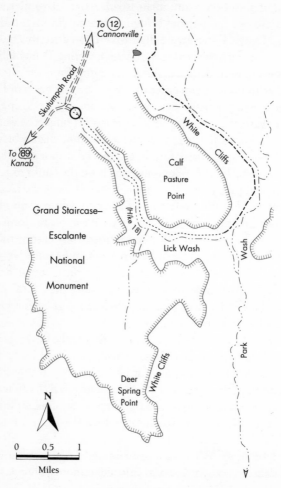

of the Grand Staircase in southern Utah. What Lick Wash lacks in notoriety is compensated for by its incomparable beauty. Indeed, it is perhaps the most scenic, and seldom-visited, canyon covered in this book.

Exciting narrow passages in the upper reaches of the canyon give way to a wider canyon below, embraced by bold Navajo Sandstone cliffs studded with tall pines, rising 600 to 800 feet to the mesa rims above. The wash is dry, and travel down its sandy and gravelly bed is easy, passable to any hiker.

Begin the hike from the end of the spur road by walking down the rock-strewn wash. Bluffs of Navajo Sandstone, studded with ponderosa pines, rise ahead, and the wash seems to disappear between them. Soon you enter the sandstone-enveloped gorge, which quickly slots up, and you make your way ahead through the narrow slickrock corridor. Within minutes you reach a short fence that spans the gap between the canyon walls. Climb over or crawl through the fence, passing the only obstacle in the canyon.

Tall pines are abundant in the canyon, and in places there are groves of Gambel oak. Tall, slender Douglas-firs and clumps of Rocky Mountain maple, vegetation more typical of much higher elevations, testify to the cool microclimate that prevails in the shady confines of the canyon.

After about 1 mile, you leave the narrow passages behind, and the canyon begins to open up, cutting through deep alluvial deposits that form benches flanking the wash, hosting a variety of shrubs and gnarled woodland trees. The canyon walls grow higher as you proceed, with smooth convex slopes of slickrock sweeping upward for hundreds of feet to the square-edged mesas above. Curved lines of cross-bedding on the slickrock shoulders reach to the base of fluted cliffs, decorated with dark black streaks and a brown patina of desert varnish. Ponderosa pines grow tall and straight at the base of the great cliffs and fringe the rims of the mesas above.

During the lower 2 miles of Lick Wash, you will find cow trails to follow, shortcutting the minor meanders of the wash via the benches above. After about 3 miles, the hulking mass of No Mans Mesa fills your view ahead. By now the arroyo of Lick Wash has grown deeper. As you approach the mouth of the wash you will spy a shallow, but obvious, alcove on the left (north) canyon wall, scooped out of a shoulder of slickrock that projects into the canyon. This is your indication that it is time to leave the arroyo, which you should do before you come abreast of the alcove.

Ascend out of the arroyo via cow trails to the north-side bench, where you will find an old four-wheel-drive track. Follow this faint doubletrack out into the valley of Park Wash, first east, then north, crossing a bench thick with the growth of big sagebrush and exotic Russian thistle (tumbleweed).

Calf Pasture Point and its sheer white cliffs loom 800 feet overhead on your left, while the equally impressive cliffs bounding No Mans Mesa define the eastern margin of the valley. These are the White Cliffs of the Grand Staircase, and they form the second tallest riser in the series of cliffs and terraces that stair-step north out of the Arizona Strip into south-central Utah.

After enjoying the dramatic landscape of the White Cliffs, return the way you came.

19
WIRE PASS TO BUCKSKIN GULCH

General description: A short but exciting day hike through the very tight narrows of Wire Pass, located in the Paria Canyon–Vermilion Cliffs Wilderness.

Distance: 3.4 miles, round-trip.

Difficulty: Easy.

Trail conditions: Wash route.

Average hiking time: 1.5 to 2 hours, round-trip.

Trailhead elevation: 4,880 feet.

Low point: 4,700 feet.

Elevation loss and gain: 180 feet.

Optimum seasons: April through early June; September through October.

Water availability: None available; bring your own.

Hazards: Flash flood danger.

Permits: Pay the appropriate fee ($5 per person/per day; $5 per dog/per day; free day use for kids 12 years or younger; and group size limit of 10 people) at the trailhead register/self-service fee station.

Topo maps: Pine Hollow Canyon (Utah-Arizona) USGS quad; BLM: Paria Canyon–Vermilion Cliffs Wilderness map, Hiker's Guide to Paria Canyon, or Kanab.

Key points:
0.0 Wire Pass Trailhead.

Wire Pass to Buckskin Gulch

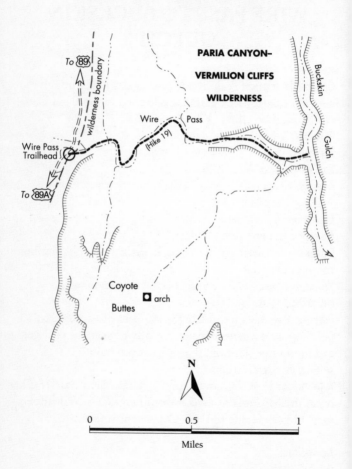

1.2 Narrows begin.
1.7 Confluence with Buckskin Gulch.

Finding the trailhead: Follow U.S. Highway 89 to an unsigned, southbound dirt road that branches off the highway at the west end of a "50 mph" right-angle curve just west of The Cockscomb. Find the turnoff 0.8 mile west of milepost 25, and 34 miles northwest of Page, Arizona, or 0.2 mile south of milepost 26, and 37.5 miles east of Kanab, Utah.

This dirt road (known as the House Rock Valley Road) is passable to cars in dry weather, barring severe runoff damage, and steadily ascends for 2.5 miles to a saddle separating The Cockscomb and Buckskin Mountain. Ignore the right fork to Fivemile Mountain at the saddle, then descend to a crossing of the Buckskin Gulch wash after 4.4 miles, where the road is subject to flood damage. The signed turnoff to Buckskin Gulch Trailhead (located 0.2 mile east of the road), which you avoid, is located a short distance south of the wash.

You reach the spacious Wire Pass Trailhead, located on the west side of the road, 8.4 miles south of US 89. Several undeveloped camping areas can be found en route to the trailhead. Pit toilets are in place at both the Buckskin Gulch and Wire Pass trailheads.

The hike: Buckskin Gulch is the ultimate in canyon country slot canyons. For 12.5 miles, the gulch is enveloped in a very narrow gorge 100 to 200 feet deep, flanked by vaulting, convoluted walls of Navajo Sandstone. Buckskin Gulch is renowned not only because of its continuous, challenging narrows, but also because there is no other canyon like it in the world.

Wire Pass, a gorge carved through The Cockscomb by Coyote Wash, is the most popular entry route into Buckskin Gulch. Wire Pass is short, but its narrows are even more confined than those in Buckskin. This is an excellent, easy hike through Wire Pass into the famous gorge of Buckskin Gulch. You can extend the day hike as far as you wish by exploring Buckskin's narrows either up-canyon or down.

As in any slot canyon, do not enter Wire Pass or Buckskin Gulch if there is the slightest chance of rainfall. In these canyons, as little as one-quarter inch of rain can run off the slickrock landscape and turn the slots into inescapable death traps. Save this memorable trip for fair weather only.

From the Wire Pass Trailhead, cross the road and follow the well-worn trail to the trailhead register and fee station. The trail ahead is well-signed and sandy as it leads to a hiker's maze in a fenceline. The maze is a V-shaped passage that allows people, but not cows, to enter Wire Pass. Here Coyote Wash carves the portal to Wire Pass through The Cockscomb, where tilted red-tinted beds of Navajo Sandstone flank the wash.

Beyond the hiker's maze, signs direct you into the wash, a wide, sandy and cobble-strewn avenue where the walking is easy, and there are few obstacles to slow you down. Be aware, however, that hiking conditions can change with the passage of each flash flood. Always check current hiking conditions at the Paria Contact Station on US 89 before entering the canyon.

Wire Pass remains wide and shallow for 1.2 miles, bounded by low slickrock bluffs and sandy slopes. The slopes north of the wash are mantled in a veneer of white rocks and cobbles, rocks of the Kaibab Limestone washed down over the ages from the slopes of broad Buckskin Mountain to the west.

Eventually, slickrock walls close in, and the wash becomes rock-strewn. Soon thereafter, at 1.2 miles, you enter the first short stretch of narrows. Beyond the confines of this constriction, you are soon swallowed up in another, very narrow slot where only 4 feet separate the canyon walls. Logs wedged between the tight, convoluted cliffs overhead are mute reminders of the tremendous force of flash floods in narrow desert canyons.

The third narrows are the deepest and most confining of all, pinching down to merely 2 feet wide in places. After exiting this final slot, you skirt a deep and shadowed alcove, then emerge into the boulder-littered wash of Buckskin Gulch. Down-canyon the walls quickly close in and Buckskin slots up. Though not as tight as Wire Pass, the gulch is still very narrow and stays that way for many miles ahead. Interesting narrows are located up-canyon as well.

When you have had enough of being swallowed up deep within this confined gorge, backtrack to more open country and the trailhead.